MAKE YOUR VOICE HEARD

MAKE YOUR VOICE HEARD

An Actor's Guide to Increased Dramatic Range Through Vocal Training

CHUCK JONES

with a Foreword by Caymichael Patten

BACK STAGE BOOKS

An imprint of Watson-Guptill Publications, New York

To Josleen Wilson, Ryland Jordan, and David Farkas, and to the memories of Beatrice A. Jones and Roy London

Copyright © 1996 by Chuck Jones
First published in 1996 in the United States by Back Stage Books, an imprint of Watson-Guptill Publications, a division of BPI Communications, Inc., 1515 Broadway, New York, NY 10036-8986.
Library of Congress Cataloging-in-Publication Data for this title can be obtained by writing to the Library of Congress, Washington, DC.

Manufactured in the United States of America
ISBN 0-8230-8333-0

1 2 3 4 5 / 00 99 98 97 96

Editor: Dale Ramsey
Designer: Jay Anning
Production Manager: Hector Campbell

He who is incapable of feeling strong passions, of being shaken by anger, or living in every sense of the word will never be a good actor.

— SARAH BERNHARDT

ACKNOWLEDGMENTS

For their encouragement, support, and assistance in the writing and development of this book, I heartily thank Caymichael Patten, Nels Hennum, Paul Lukas, Dale Ramsey, Gloria Hale, Faith Hamlin, Anne Cairns, Sue Walker, Ziva Kwitney, Tanya Berezin, Adina Porter, Keith Cobb, Michael Howard, Lilene Mansell, Patsy Rodenburg, Elizabeth Himmelstein, and Judy Vivier. And all of the many people who helped me that I may have neglected to mention.

CONTENTS

A Note to My Readers

The exercises described in this book have been used by thousands of actors. If any exercises cause discomfort, eliminate them from your practice. Please see your physician and get his or her approval on the exercises.

CHUCK JONES

FOREWORD

BY CAYMICHAEL PATTEN
Director, the Caymichael Patten Studio

I first met Chuck Jones when I was a young director coaching an actress for an audition for The Actor's Studio. The scene was from *The Country Girl*. Her partner was Chuck. Both of them were more experienced than I was, so I was nervous, but I blossomed working with Chuck. He may not have known it, but he was teaching even then. That was when I was first exposed to the way he could put his whole concentration on someone, with open attention, without judgment, listening for the essential. Guess what? My notes to these actors got better, because I could pick out what was germane in what I was trying to say—because that's what Chuck was responding to.

I've seen that kind of attention when he was talking to a new student, who had come to class complaining, "I've never been able to breathe right and act at the same time." Chuck zeroed in on this fellow and said, "What is breathing right? There's no special voice-class breathing or proper acting breathing. One of the ways we know what's happening with people is how they take a breath."

I could see the actor's face soften as it dawned on him that Chuck's work wasn't going to be the typical voice-class hokum, that it emphasized connecting the actor's voice to his or her emotional life. That's what we all recognize as truthfulness.

So I've sent him many students over the years, saying to them, "If you think this work has nothing to do with your acting, you're wrong. Do the exercises, and your acting will get better." And it does. They come away from his work more in touch with themselves, more relaxed, more deeply connected emotionally, more responsive to their core acting selves.

I hope I'm communicating what a terrific teacher he is and what a boon his work is to the actor. If you can't study with him directly, or if you have worked with him and need a reminder, this book is for you.

PREFACE: VOICE TRAINING AND SPEECH TRAINING

What can this approach to voice training do for the actor? Partially, the answer depends on the state of your voice (and your vocal awareness) at this moment. You are each one of you different, and you will have different vocal problems and strengths. People also have varying levels of ambition and discipline. The results will be unique for each person.

I can promise you this—that if you read and understand this book and do the exercises on a regular basis, ten to fifteen minutes every day, your voice will improve a great deal. And it will be *your voice,* not an imitation of someone else's voice.

Actors who follow my advice have often told me that:

- Their voices improve in power and range.

- They have more vocal stamina.

- They are more focused in their acting.

- The honesty of their acting has grown and, in fact, their ability to act well has strengthened.

- Their auditions have gotten better results and are more satisfying.

- Other people often respond quite differently to them. Women, especially, tell me they are taken more seriously.

This may seem too good to be true. But these are real comments from actors I have taught.

But let me *stress*, there is no magic here. The exercises are not miracles—just very effective, if done regularly. They take a little bit of time to work, but are surprisingly quick. The vocal work I ask you to do is a very natural process of development. Many images are used, but the exercises are physiologically sound. Your voice will grow in stages, much like a seed grows when it is placed in the soil. This approach does work; I have seen it work for twenty years with thousands of actors.

My approach is a very individual and unique view of voice training. It is all based on my personal experiences teaching privately, in studios and in conservatory Bachelor of Fine Arts and Master of Fine Arts programs, as well as on my fifteen years of acting professionally. This is not a "middle of the road" approach to voice training, and there are those who will not agree with my methods. The bottom line, to me, is plainly and simply the results you achieve. No matter how terrific an approach is or seems to be, if it doesn't yield good and reliable results for you, it is not effective.

My method is very much a "cut to the chase" approach. This is basically a book containing the quickest, most effective exercises I know. The ideas I've written about may very well be quite different from what you've been exposed to before. In this book, I have cut out anything that I feel is not important, that is of minor interest, and that is, in my opinion, counterproductive.

Let me tell you a little bit more about voice work.

In many countries, voice and speech are taught together by the same acting teacher. In the United States, the two are often taught separately and by different specialists. Many actors are confused by the differences between voice and speech work. An actor recently telephoned me and said, "My acting teacher told me to work on my voice, so I want to take your speech class." I explained to him that I teach voice, and that voice training is not the same as speech training.

Voice training primarily deals with the production of vocal tone—the range, openness, expressiveness, and flexibility of the actor's voice. Speech training concentrates primarily on articulation, dialect, and scansion. They do, of course, overlap. Both often incorporate breathing, physical relaxation, and emotional work. And both kinds of training are equally important to the actor.

Vocal exercises accomplish two important goals for the actor: They develop the vocal instrument, and they put the actor in touch with his or her emotional center—that is, the actor learns to allow the voice to express his or her emotional life.

As far as speech training goes, in my experience the approach used by Edith Skinner from the 1940s through 1970 is the most valuable and practical method for the actor. Skinner taught in major conservatory training programs in the United States. She explained her method in her book *Speak with Distinction,* which has been republished (in 1990) in an edition prepared by speech teachers Lilene Mansell and Timothy Monich.

My approach to voice training is based generally on the method devised by Iris Warren, a renowned British voice teacher who passed away in 1963. I first learned her exercises from Kristin Linklater, founder of the Working Theater, which trained voice, acting, and movement teachers in the 1970s. Over the years I have explored many other approaches to voice training and have found that Warren's approach was consistently more productive than any other, but I also realized that I could use all of my experience as an actor and teacher to make this approach more uniquely my own and, in my opinion, more effective.

Voice training is not unlike learning any new skill. You cannot study voice passionately for a certain period and then stop. Indeed, you can never *learn* it; you can only exercise it, and the major benefits will continue only as long as you continue to practice.

The key to successful voice training is consistency. Over the years I have learned two important facts:

- The exercises must be effective and clear. The individual goals of each exercise must be understandable to the student.

- The exercises must also produce very quick results. Progress must be experienced from the start.

Thus my goal as a teacher has been to develop time-efficient exercises—effective and fast-working. Over time, I have changed the exercises I use considerably in order to make them more understandable and, therefore, more accessible. The voice workout presented in this book (Chapter 8) has been especially formulated, in terms of time and sequence, to support the contemporary American style of acting and actor training. I've provided the basics of voice training in a simple—although not simplistic—regimen known to produce results.

As you train your voice, I hope one of your goals will be to change very strong lifelong physical habits of containing excessive tensions in the body. These habits have usually resulted in vocal limitations. Indeed, you have probably been reinforcing poor vocal habits (without knowing it) for much of your life, and it will take daily, regular work to effect change. Habits can work for you as well as against you. This book is about forming new, beneficial ones.

But can you learn voice training from a book? Yes! That, obviously, was part of my overall goal as an author. From my one-year professional voice-training program I have distilled this basic workout for presentation in book form, and it covers all the major areas of vocal development. As presented in these pages, these twenty exercises can be self-taught and used by beginners and advanced students. This workout will change your voice.

I believe it's critical for actors to understand all the elements of their craft and to be able to work on them on their own. Sometimes, it seems to me that voice and acting teachers intentionally try to keep their work mysterious. When this happens, actors feel they must study forever with this or that particular teacher or stop doing the work altogether. The more mysterious or vague voice training seems, the less actors feel they can master it. This makes it practically impossible for them to work on their own. This can also result in becoming dependent on the teacher.

When you yourself understand what you are doing and why, you can take responsibility for your work and change whatever you need to. Every time you take on a new role, you will feel secure enough to explore it through your voice, expand your performance, and realize the part to its fullest potential.

Voice training today is about feeling confident that your vocal instrument will respond to the emotion you are trying to express and operate effectively. In my teaching, I distinguish between being "in control" and being "in charge." Voice training is not about controlling the sounds you make. It is about being confidently in charge. If something starts to go wrong with your voice, as a professional actor you should know how to fix it. Then you are in charge. The more confident you feel, the freer both your speech and your acting become.

Whenever you have an opportunity to study voice with a good voice teacher, I hope you will take advantage of it. I feel that the exercises featured in this book are compatible with any effective voice-training class you might take in the United States or in England. Almost every good teacher adheres to the same principles, although emphasis, specific combinations, and sequences of exercises will vary. These exercises are also compatible with various acting approaches. Professional actors usually know what they need to work on, and they also know whether a particular teacher or particular method is helping them. In the course of your career, I hope you will be confident enough to take what you need from each teacher you consult. I also hope you take what you can from this book and that it will open your eyes to some new ways of looking at voice and actor training.

1

INTRODUCTION

When I was teaching at the California Institute of the Arts, in Valencia, in the 1970s, I was surprised to find that many of my students thought they didn't need voice training because they intended to work in television and film. They assumed voice training dealt with stage projection only. I realized then that before they could benefit from my classes I needed to explain what voice training was all about.

First of all, it isn't just the projection of the voice from the stage, although actors who work to develop their vocal instrument automatically increase their capacity to be heard. Modern voice training is far from the dogmatic, repetitious, irritating type of work associated with a "stagy" voice. Effective voice training is about being *expressive.*

Today, actors must be able to use their voices in a wide variety of situations—in small theaters, huge barn-like arenas with harsh amplification, in television studios, on feature-film sound stages and on-location film sites. Actors may work in situations where electronic amplification blows their voice out of human proportion, and in situations where there is no sound enhancement at all. They may record their lines in a studio completely unrelated to the actual scene in which their image will finally appear. Something unique to modern-day actors is giving live interviews on television talk shows. It is impossible (even if it were desirable) to employ a different voice or different vocal technique for each of these situations. In each situation the actor needs his or her voice to be fully responsive, with the appropriate level of loudness, range, emotion, and quality. An actor's job is to express every kind of emotion, in virtually every kind of environment imaginable, when he or she chooses.

In the recent past many actors were known for having a "beautiful voice," a "stage voice," a "cute voice," a "funny voice," or a particular sound they had been taught to copy. Sally Struthers used a little squeak in the television series *All in the Family*. Richard Burton's voice was so "beautiful" that it sometimes got in his way.

Similarly, some actors like the idea of having a voice that is idiosyncratic and attention-getting. Think of the offbeat sounds of Carol Channing and Tammy Grimes. Such voices can attract a lot of notice, but their odd quality can end up being a liability, making it impossible for the actor to be cast as a normal human being. I have seen cases of this many times. One actress who had a funny vocal twist came to me to "fix" it because she was consistently being type-cast as a kook. She remembered the moment in her first play when she got a laugh on a straight line merely because of the sound of her voice, and she had been relying on this ever since. Eventually she found her voice too limiting and wanted to be more vocally honest. We worked on developing the range and power of her voice, and she soon became comfortable using many different levels in her voice.

An actor's voice, then, should never stand out as a separate part of the actor's performance. The purpose of training is to make the voice an expressive instrument.

Many actors reject all voice training. Some people think their voices are like their height: At a certain age it becomes fixed. You may not be able to grow taller after a certain point in your life, but you can always develop your voice. In fact, the voice isn't even fully mature until after age forty, and it is capable of change throughout your life. The choice does not have to be between a phony voice or no voice at all. You can train your voice to be more resonant, stronger, more personal, and more open.

All of this will make you a better actor. However, many actors, as well as acting teachers and directors, believe that the microphone—whether on stage or just beyond camera range—will solve all vocal problems. Unfortunately, a sound system can only amplify whatever is vocally already there. Amplification cannot make a lusterless voice more expressive or a weak voice more powerful.

Several seasons ago, a long-awaited play, directed by one of America's most important stage and film directors, opened on Broadway. Three famous American film stars appeared in the leading roles, a rare event on Broadway. However, even though the show was well miked, the voices of the stars fairly ruined their acting and almost destroyed the production. During the play's most dramatic moments, the audience could be heard clearing their throats and coughing. Why?

On a subconscious level, audiences pick up all kinds of information from the way actors use their voices. In this case, at the play's climaxes, vocal and emotional power was implied but not actually present. The actors were pushing. The audience, in turn, sensed the strain and reacted by clearing their own throats. (In the same way, if an actor is holding his or her breath onstage, audience members will hold their breath, too.)

Truthfully speaking, when actors strain trying to produce power, they communicate weakness rather than strength. Pushing can never adequately substitute for power. When an actor wants a character to be strong, he or she must have a strong instrument. It can't be faked.

YOUR VOCAL INSTRUMENT

The sole purpose of the actor's voice is to communicate. Central to conveying to the audience everything the actor is thinking and feeling, the voice should have a developed range; it can be powerful and strong when necessary, and it can be personal and intimate at other times.

What happens if you are cast in a role that demands that you grow from a flirtatious, carefree youth into a violent, imperious monarch? You can change your attitude and your motivation. You can change your costume and makeup. But unless your vocal instrument has range and resonance and is responsive, your voice will remain the same. Think of the result if an actress like Melanie Griffith or Mariel Hemingway tried to play Catherine the Great. Physically, both of these women are big and beautiful, but their voices could belong to children. (To give due credit, Hemingway has done a good job of developing the resonance and range of a voice that Woody Allen said sounded like Minnie Mouse.)

A fully developed instrument is important for other reasons. Actors who develop serious vocal problems because of weak voices that become strained may be replaced in a play or a film. It costs too much money to postpone a theatrical opening or a film shoot so that they can recover their voices or get some remedial training.

Your performance will be more effective if you are free from vocal worries, for actors must be physically released, even in extreme physical conditions, to be emotionally revealing. Actor Jeff Daniels was once preparing a demanding one-man show based on Dalton Trumbo's novel *Johnny Got His Gun* at Circle Repertory Company, in New York. The character has a head, but no body, and the play's action takes place in his mind. This production involved unorthodox, stylized physical staging, and throughout the play, Jeff had to climb all over the stage. As the day of dress rehearsal neared, his voice began to disappear. Jeff is a disciplined actor, interested in every facet of theatrical artistry. Because of previous voice work, he recognized a potentially serious vocal problem in the making. He asked me to observe a rehearsal to try to identify its source.

The complicated blocking, combined with the strenuous vocal demands of the part, was creating extreme physical tension in Jeff's body, particularly around his upper back and shoulders. Also, he was not breathing fully. He and I went through the blocking step by step and concentrated on eliminating the severe tension around his neck. We also made sure that the breathing was full. That solved the problem, and his voice was fine throughout the run.

Actors are often subjected to similar kinds of physical and emotional stress, particularly when making movies and rehearsing plays, when the same show-stopping scene must be continually repeated until it is perfect. The physical tension that arises from playing intensely emotional scenes is also a common problem. Intense emotion creates physical tension, which in turn causes vocal problems. The goal is to relax physically, without reducing emotional intensity. All these problems can be solved with effective voice training.

Even a well-trained voice can get into trouble. Chris Fields, another very talented actor, was once rehearsing to play the lead in *Home Front* on Broadway. Chris had one very emotional scene in the last act which required him to rapidly shout "Shut up!" twenty times with intensity. For several weeks the director rehearsed this particular scene over and over again. Not surprisingly, Chris started to lose his voice.

Like Jeff Daniels, Chris knew he was headed toward serious vocal problems, but he couldn't tell the director he didn't want to rehearse anymore. This was an emergency.

We ran the scene, and I could see that every time Chris shouted "Shut up!" his neck became rigid and he had to push his voice. The more he shouted, the greater the tension in his neck. The greater the tension, the more he pushed, and the weaker and raspier his voice became. To have adequate vocal strength and yet retain his emotional intensity, Chris needed to relax his neck. Believe it or not, there are specific voice exercises that help an actor accomplish this seemingly contradictory task. Chris concentrated on those particular exercises every day for several weeks. He went on to be brilliant and very moving in the role, and he was able to sustain eight performances a week for the run of the play.

Every actor should learn to trouble-shoot his or her own vocal instrument (see Chapter 11, "Dealing with Common Problems"). When you understand how your instrument works, you will also have a good idea of how to identify problems and correct them when things start to go wrong.

CARING FOR THE VOICE

I once acted in Michael Weller's *Moonchildren* at the Royal Court Theatre, in London, where the play was called *Cancer*. One scene required that I be drenched with water from head to foot. The theater was cool backstage, and the combination of cold and dampness was making my sinuses congested. I was aware of the mechanisms involved and able to trouble-shoot for myself at least enough to take the steps of drying off completely after the nightly drenching and wearing a heavy sweater between my scenes. The most important self-help was doing additional voice exercises to keep the sinus resonators clear.

Many actors, including Helen Hayes, have had vocal and allergic problems with the dust and molds that accumulate backstage in older theaters. In fact, Miss Hayes retired from theater work because of her allergies, although she continued to work in film and television until her death.

I once rehearsed a Broadway play at the New Amsterdam Roof on 42nd Street, a space which had not been used since Florenz Ziegfeld staged his *Midnight Frolics* there in the 1920s. Although historically fascinating, the theater was a nightmare as far as dust and dirt were concerned. We coughed and sneezed our way through rehearsals.

This problem is not always easily solved. It usually requires some combination of allergy medication, the ability to do effective vocal warm-ups, keeping a vaporizer in your dressing room, or just breathing steam deeply over the sink for a few minutes while running hot water. You usually have to find your own way, but knowledge and awareness of your voice are the keys.

Many other factors can affect an actor's voice: heightened language demands (as in the Greeks, Shakespeare, Molière), nervous tension in performance, and individual vocal and physical habits.

Although it's not commonly recognized, voice training does much more than solve vocal problems: Voice training allows actors to extend their range, develop power, and create that mysterious quality known as presence. Voice training helps put actors in touch with their deepest emotional states and allows them to connect to their roles in a profound way. And voice training helps actors develop the capacity to reveal the full range of their inner lives. This sounds like a lot, but it is indeed the truth. I know of no better way to make a person into an honest, revealing, and interesting actor than to work effectively with his or her voice.

More of what voice training can do for you, as well as the techniques you can use to develop your own instrument, will be explored in the succeeding chapters.

2

LOOKING BACK, LOOKING FORWARD

I have found that there is very little specific information about actors' voices down through the ages. One reason, I am sure, is that in the past it was assumed that an actor had an effective voice, or he or she wouldn't have been able to be an actor—just as a physically awkward person would probably not be a dancer. Voice is always emphasized, but details are hard to come by, in the historical accounts.

I have learned that the vocal usage of the actor was connected to the style and form of the text. The formality of early material certainly led to a measured quality in the actor's voice and breathing. Vocal presentation, in the early theater, was probably much closer to singing and chanting than what we call acting today.

Whatever the material requires, the actor must supply—especially vocally. (This is a fact that many contemporary actors fail to recognize.) If the writing is formal, perhaps in a strict meter, then more than likely the breathing will be controlled, the voice will be placed and, probably, highly manipulated, and the whole style of the actor's performance will be more presentational than we are used to.

Remember that the definition of, and our views about, acting are in constant change. The recordings we now hear of Sarah Bernhardt (1844–1923) sound extremely theatrical and presentational, if not downright phony. But in her time, the same performance was thought to be shocking in its naturalism. Acting (and voice usage) is not a static thing.

It is odd that "naturalism" always pops up as a standard for judging an actor's performance—no matter how theatrical, presentational, and formal the style may be. I have often thought that perhaps what has been called naturalism is really an actor's ability to be honest, no matter what the style of performance requires. Through the ages, actors have commonly been judged by the quality of their voices as well as the naturalism they exhibit in their acting. What audiences consider "natural" and "real" has varied widely over time and continues to change. Thus the actor's craft has consisted of certain elements that have never changed, but the training an actor needs has been periodically redefined.

THE EARLIEST STAGES

Acting may have begun as early as 4,000 B.C., when Egyptian priests worshipped the memory of the dead in theatrical rituals. The first nonreligious acting may have developed in China, where professional players acted out stories about the current emperor's dead ancestors. We know little of how the actors of ancient cultures worked, but acting has probably always been an art of remembering.

The actors of Classical Greece, burdened with heavy costumes and enormous masks, presumably depended on full body posturing and distinctive hand gestures to communicate the passions of gods and human beings. Movement was evidently stately and formal. One famous incident of which we do know, which concerns the actor Polus, tells us something about the Greek actor's desire to convey emotional truth. When Polus played Electra he carried the ashes of his own dead son onstage. In the scene when Electra laments the fate of her dead brother, Orestes, Polus embraced the urn of his son's ashes as if it held those of Orestes and poured out genuine grief.

Greek theater began when dancing actors, accompanied by the music of a lyre, sang passionate hymns, or dithyrambs, at harvest festivals in honor of Dionysus, the god of wine and fertility. These performances were eventually staged in huge open-air theaters with a semicircular seating area built into a hillside. A flat circular area below the first row of seats was cut out for dancers and singers, with a raised stage behind it for actors.

According to legend, Thespis, a choral leader of the sixth century B.C., became the first actor when he assumed the part of the leading character in a dithyrambic song honoring Dionysus. Thespis spoke and the chorus responded. Aristotle tells us that other actors and characters were added, and drama began to develop. Playwrights emerged to provide texts, and the actors' roles grew larger.

In these roughly carved theaters, thousands watched the great plays of the classical period of Greece. Because subtle gestures and facial expressions were lost in the vastness of the arenas, Greek actors therefore paid much attention to developing an expressive, well-trained voice. Aristotle gave us a clue to this when he defined acting as "the right management of the voice to express the various emotions."

But though this era seems to be the start of a lot of attention to the voice, much of it is confusing to us now. The actors wore masks, but did the masks contain megaphones? The ancient Greek theaters that have survived have extremely fine acoustics, according to Helen Hayes and others. Yet there are stories of Greek actors cutting the back of their tongues to create a larger sound. It sounds awful to me—but who knows? (Centuries later, Stanley, a notorious singing teacher, used metal instruments to force the tongue to release. He was called, by some, "the butcher of voice," and the voice produced by such methods was big and empty—devoid of emotional connection and subtlety, in my view.) My friend Patsy Rodenburg, the voice and speech coach of the Royal National Theatre in London, attended a lecture on ancient Greek acting and learned that the exercises they did are similar to what we do today. That rings true to me.

Ancient actors would have practiced constantly to increase the efficiency of their vocal production. Perhaps they did gain additional vocal resonance by wearing those larger-than-life hollow masks, which also increased visibility and identified the character to the audience. (Changing masks allowed one actor to play several parts.)

Poetic and operatic qualities in Greek tragedies demanded that the actor be able to sing as well as to recite verse. Not only musical training, but detailed study of enunciation, timing, and rhythmic perfection were required.

The Greek theaters that still stand today were not built until the fourth century B.C. Row upon row of stone tiers encircling and rising above the performance area in a concave pocket reflected sound and created those remarkable acoustics. In the theater at Epidaurus, for example, a match struck in the orchestra can be heard in the farthest seat.

THE ROMAN AND MEDIEVAL STAGE

The Romans modeled their theaters after those of the Greeks, but made them much smaller—from 200 to 1,500 seats. Roman players improvised their plays, using the individual idiosyncracies of their characters as a starting point. The ancient Roman actors live for us in the words of poets and orators who admired them and studied their art. For centuries afterward, actors used Horace's lines to bolster their belief in emotional realism: "If you would have me weep, you must first of all feel grief yourself." This may have been a major change in acting technique.

Acting flourished as the virtuosity of the individual actor was admired. With the collapse of the Roman Empire, theater fell into the hands of wandering minstrels whose comic antics kept alive the tradition of professional acting.

Throughout the Middle Ages, professional actors struggled against Church suppression. Persistent troupes of performers—comedians and mimes, jugglers and acrobats—wandered from town to town, offering entertainment in village streets and in the courts of the great lords. Eventually, theater was accepted in the Church in the form of pageants that were usually performed by local people.

THE RENAISSANCE

Acting styles have always been influenced by the playwright's imagination, as well as by changes in society. In the new humanism of the Renaissance, plays moved out of the churches into the courts of the aristocracy. Technical innovations altered performing styles. The proscenium arch, elaborate costumes, mechanical devices, and painted scenery dominated courtly productions, while tumblers and jugglers continued working in the village squares. From these strolling players came the acting tradition known as *commedia dell' arte all' improviso*—the art of improvised comedy. A dell'arte company consisted of ten or twelve players who improvised words and actions to fill in standard plot outlines. Each actor developed one stock character who had a standard costume and obvious personal traits. The Doctor, for example, always dressed in black and talked in a high-pitched, formal manner. Each actor spent his or her professional life perfecting one of these stage figures. Harlequin, Pierrot, and Pulcinella were famous dell' arte characters. These companies established basic rules of language, voice, and gesture that generations of professional actors adopted and now take for granted: planning exits, waiting for other actors to finish speaking, falling silent when another actor enters and begins to speak, and so on.

Actors came to emerge as individual artists. Roving troupes were replaced by resident acting companies, and actors individually began to achieve fame. Unknown authors of religious pageants were replaced by such great names as Ariosto, Lope de Vega, Marlowe, and Shakespeare. In the hands of these playwrights, actors faced the problem of portraying individuals rather than stock characters; staged drama had become the art of expressing individual passion. London's famous Globe Theatre opened in 1599; Shakespeare's *Julius Caesar* was one of its first productions, and the theater staged the first performances of many of Shakespeare's plays.

Shakespeare was an actor in the Globe's resident company, the Lord Chamberlain's men, later known as the King's

Men. The theater itself was a hexagonal building with an inner court measuring about 55 feet across. The audience either stood in the open courtyard or sat in one of three semicircular galleries. More than 1,500 people could crowd into the space. A platform stage with three levels stretched halfway into the court. With so many stage spaces, the multiple scenes of Shakespeare's plays could be played through without interruption for scenery changes.

Elizabethan acting was probably not realistic in the modern sense, but actors playing Shakespearean roles had to understand the motives of their characters and the psychology behind the action. The emphasis was on admirable vocal delivery and appropriate gestures to give expression to the poet's words.

ACTORS OF PROMINENCE

In England, theater during the Restoration period was limited to two London playhouses—the Duke's Theatre and the Theatre Royal—which were simply long halls with a stage at one end. The physical layout precluded spectacular production values, and so actors became the theater's dominant element. The Elizabethan legacy of portraying people with complex emotions was gradually enriched by a series of brilliant English and Continental actors. One assumes today that their voices served them well.

Among the actors who achieved prominence in the 1700s were Colley Cibber, Anne Oldfield, Charles Macklin, Peg Woffington, and John Philip Kemble and his sister, Sarah Siddons. The best known actor, David Garrick (1717–79), is still regarded as one of the greatest in the history of the British theater. Noted for his naturalness, vivacity, and powerful characterizations, Garrick played tragedy, comedy, and farce with equal skill, including in his wide repertory seventeen Shakespearean roles, among them Hamlet, Lear, Macbeth, and Benedick. When he produced a celebration at Stratford-on-Avon to commemorate the 200th anniversary of Shakespeare's birth, Garrick made Shakespearean drama popular again.

Two great theaters were built in Garrick's time, the Drury Lane and the Covent Garden. The Drury Lane originally seated about 2,000. In 1791, Richard Brinsley Sheridan had it torn it down and rebuilt to seat 3,500. The hugeness of the theaters no doubt contributed to a full-blown acting style marked by exaggerated volume and resonance and unnatural voice and speech patterns.

During the 1800s, actors continued to dominate the stage: Edmund Kean, Ellen Terry, and Henry Irving in England; Edwin Forrest and Edwin Booth in the United States. Forrest, born in Philadelphia in 1806, was the first native-born theatrical star in the United States. Today he is remembered primarily for his passionate renderings of Othello, Lear, and Richard III. The somewhat younger Joseph Jefferson (1829–1905), also born in Philadelphia, came from a family of English actors. Jefferson's most famous role was the title character in the long-running production of *Rip Van Winkle.*

Both of these famous American actors were eclipsed by Edwin Booth. Booth was born into a theatrical family in 1833. His father was the well-known Junius Brutus Booth, and his younger brother the assassin John Wilkes Booth. Edwin became the foremost American tragedian of his day. He was so gifted that he won fame in England, playing all the great Shakespearean roles, notably Lear, Othello, Richard III, Shylock, Macbeth, and Hamlet. (For New York actors interested in theater history, Edwin Booth left his house on New York's

Gramercy Park to the Players Club, a theatrical club which he co-founded with Mark Twain. Today, his room on the third floor remains untouched, and his brokenhearted letter apologizing to the American people for the acts of his brother can be found in the library.)

In France, actors François Talma and Sarah Bernhardt dazzled audiences. Bernhardt achieved her first big success when she recited the choruses in Racine's *Athalie* using in her celebrated "voice of gold." In addition to her superior vocal qualities, Bernhardt was dedicated to every aspect of actor training. She wrote voluminously on the subject of acting, emphasizing that actors must do everything in their power to achieve truth in their characters, including studying history, background, emotions, and the playwright's intent. She said that the actor's imagination "must play freely, and he must not feel hampered in the expansion of his nature." She asked: "How can he [the actor] convince another of his emotion, of the sincerity of his passions, if he is unable to convince himself. . . ? If he is not shaken by anger, and if pity does not move him profoundly, he will appear insipid. To be worthy of the name an actor must be capable of a continuous dissection of his personality" (*The Art of the Theater,* 1924).

Naturalism in acting was one of Bernhardt's favorite subjects: "If you would be natural, you must avoid the persistent mannerisms that actors frequently adopt believing they please the public. In the end these become merely bad habits. . . . It is true that the more one attempts to define what is natural, the more one perceives the difficulty of squeezing it into a brief and simple formula."

In the theater of her day, Bernhardt's only rival was the Italian actress Eleanora Duse (1859–1924), who for many years was considered her inferior. Duse was fourteen when she first played Juliet, in Verona. As she matured into a sad, expressive, beautiful woman, she developed an artistry so original and mysterious that critics were at a loss to describe it. Of her the American dramatist Stark Young wrote: "Duse could never be a school or a craft, her method was herself. She had no tricks, no efforts to attract or pique or impress, but only the desire to exist in the life to which she had given herself for those two hours on the stage, only the desire to convey to us and to confirm for herself the infinity of living within the woman she portrayed there."

MODERN ACTING AND TRAINING

Despite Bernhardt's advocacy of naturalism, Duse was the only actor of her era to completely abandon traditional artifice and declamation, thus establishing a modern acting style to suit modern drama. In the summer of 1897, Bernhardt induced Duse to perform in her theater in Paris, in the role of Camille, one of Bernhardt's own triumphal roles. For several weeks, the two actors went head to head, and that season in Paris culminated in a gala performance, as a memorial to the playwright Alexandre Dumas *fils,* both actresses performing on the same night.

Since that event, comparisons of the two great actresses have become part of theater lore. Bernard Shaw was more impressed with Duse: "I should say without qualification that it is the best modern acting I have ever seen." Duse became the ideal interpreter of the ground-breaking playwrights of the late 1800s and early decades of the 1900s, among them Henrik Ibsen and Gabriele D'Annunzio.

The course of drama in the twentieth century was being set at this time. In 1866, George II, the Duke of Saxe-Meiningen, organized a company devoted to the principle that the primary purpose of production is to give a true and faithful rendering of the play. There would be no star actors, and the entire ensemble would "play together like an orchestra." Following Saxe-Meiningen's principles, André Antoine established the Théâtre-Libre in Paris, and Konstantin Stanislavski established the Moscow Art Theater. In turn, these companies led to new theater groups in many countries.

The story of twentieth-century acting may be summed up as the attempt to rediscover an *inner truth* in performance. This was consistent with the cultivation of a naturalistic style by figures like Duse, but it was not necessarily the result of it. Numerous times in the history of the theater, the ability to imitate the outward gestures and mannerisms of real people was considered the only approach to acting a part. Of course, physical skills—mastery over a well-developed voice and body—had been recognized since ancient times as essential to an actor, and through the ages an externals-based performance style was often the standard. It has been commonly believed that if external characteristics were allowed to be natural, the inner magic of the actor would be able to shine through. In other words, using various physical traits, makeup, and so on, helps actors make an internal, emotional connection that fills out the idea of the character.

The advantage of this *outside/in* approach was that it could be taught and learned in a systematic way. It could also be seen and heard by the audience. (Actors and historians refer to the "outside/in" and "inside/out" approaches to acting; I see the distinction as being fairly artificial. I believe that actors use both approaches and that their voices reflect that. "Talent" is often the ingredient that makes any approach work and makes the voice honest and moving.)

In the hands of a gifted actor, polished outside/in technique could be transformed into great acting. Paul Muni and Laurence Olivier are famous examples of actors who used this approach to remarkably successful effect. Olivier used to start building his characters by putting on nose putty. When he played Othello, he did voice exercises to temporarily lower his voice six notes. But in lesser hands, the outside/in approach often seems mechanical and stagy and fails to touch the audience emotionally.

Perfection with the outside/in approach is rarely attained today, although some American actors continue to study the Delsarte method, based on the teachings of a nineteenth-century French actor, François Delsarte. In the early 1800s, the young Delsarte lost his voice as a result of faulty instruction. This shattering experience led him to years of diligent study, during which he observed that the body under stress or influenced by the emotions instinctively takes on the appropriate attitude or gesture. "Gesture," he wrote, "corresponds to the soul, to the heart." Delsarte believed that gesture, rather than language, was the dominant factor in conveying emotion to the audience. He turned his observations into precise laws of gesture and speech to help actors deliver more realistic performances. Delsarte taught that the body was divided into the mental, emotional, and physical—including eyeballs and eyelids. Certain positions indicated anger, rage, joy, or pleasure. The outward gesture, he said, was supposed to be "an echo of the inward gesture which gave birth to it." Thus, the gestures he taught were extremely subtle, and audiences were supposed to notice them only on a subliminal level.

Delsarte had many celebrated pupils, and his influence on acting styles in nineteenth-century France was considerable. However, by the time he died, in 1871, his method had become as elaborate and as rigid as those he had originally tried to break away from. At the beginning of the twentieth century, however, his ideas, as reinterpreted by other teachers, had a tremendous vogue in the United States. Actors who successfully used the Delsarte system practiced it until it was so fully integrated into their performances that the seams didn't show. (If you know what to look for, you can still recognize the Delsarte work in film performances of Katharine Hepburn, Helen Hayes, and Humphrey Bogart.) Some actors still find it useful to spend time on the Delsarte method in an effort to understand how every part of the body can be incorporated into expressing the emotional truth of a character.

Today, the modern science of recognizing "body language"—the psychological significance of gestures and body movements—is called *kinesics*. The problem is that if the actor does not arduously practice every single motion until it is smooth and fully integrated, he or she may have to stop and think before doing any action or movement. Acting styles have always been influenced by new technology, new playwrights, and new understanding of the human condition. For example, improved acoustical design affected the way actors presented their characters. Simultaneously, political and social developments led playwrights like Ibsen, Chekhov, and Shaw to examine more closely the motivations of their characters and place them in realistic situations and settings. Accordingly, in the modern era, major changes in acting came out of ensembles dedicated to current psychological and political ideas.

THE STANISLAVSKI SYSTEM: A TURNING POINT

In Russia, Konstantin Stanislavski (1863–1938) insisted that actors identify with their roles by becoming totally involved in the inner lives of their characters. In the modern spirit, he viewed theater as a medium through which he could educate the public about social themes. In 1897, with the writer and director Vladimir Nemirovich-Danchenko, Stanislavski formed the Moscow Art Theater, a company of actors which functioned as an organic, living unit. In producing Chekhov's *The Sea Gull* and other plays they advanced the cause of truthful, naturalistic interpretation. In fact, the Moscow Art Theater's productions of Chekhov put the company on the world's theatrical map.

Stanislavski realized that actors needed more than realistic furniture and costumes to play realistic characters. They needed an acting style that allowed them to feel and express real emotions. He set about developing the first systematic approach to reaching the actor's inner life. Stanislavski's system was not a series of rules; rather it taught actors what to do consciously so that they can be free and spontaneously emotional. They learn to use *affective memory,* or emotional substitution, to deal consciously with that part of themselves which normally remain unconscious. Stanislavski borrowed from late nineteenth-century French psychology for his ideas about the recreation of past emotions by recalling sensory detail. The important aspects of Stanislavski's system were learning to relax; avoiding distraction; developing the imagination and one's memory of sensory details; and believing in the imagined truth of the stage (he called this the magic or creative "if").

The Moscow Art Theater regularly toured the United States and had a profound influence on American directors. In New York, the young actor–director Lee Strasberg was one of these directors. A member of the Theater Guild in the 1920s, Strasberg first learned of Stanislavski's principles at the

American Laboratory Theatre. He formed the Group Theater in 1931, an ensemble company that comprised outstanding young actors working in collaboration with older, more experienced actors. Through acting, directing, and teaching, they deeply influenced American theater. Like Stanislavski's company, the Group Theater believed in acting as a means of promoting social change.

The brilliant actress Stella Adler, a member of the company and the daughter of the classical Yiddish actors Jacob and Sara Adler, gained her reputation in such Group Theater productions as *The House of Connelly* and *Awake and Sing!* in the 1930s.

Adler briefly studied with Stanislavski himself, in 1934. In 1949, a year after Strasberg became the artistic director of the Actors Studio, Adler founded her own studio, the Stella Adler Conservatory of Acting. She and Strasberg transformed the Stanislavski system into Method acting, creating a new approach to American acting.

These two innovators differed considerably on their interpretations of the Method. Adler stressed the actor's use of imagination, while Strasberg instructed actors to draw from their experiences. The common thread is that both taught actors to begin their work from within themselves. These two great teachers tutored two generations of sterling performers, including Maureen Stapleton, Marlon Brando, Shelley Winters, Warren Beatty, Robert De Niro, and many others.

AMERICAN VOICE TRAINING PIONEERS

It is assumed that, through the ages, emphasis was always placed on having an impressive and effective voice. Until this century, there is no knowledge available of any training methods. Perhaps actors in the past were chosen because they had naturally good voices. My guess is that they must have.

Now things change, and we seem to have "voice teachers." According to my research, this is the first point in recent history when actors sought out nonactors for instruction. Two teachers, or coaches, Margaret Carrington and Frances Robinson-Duff, represent a whole new phenomenon in acting.

When John Barrymore first became a leading man on Broadway, he had lazy diction and the vocal resonance of a comb-and-paper kazoo. Nevertheless, the young actor had scored with audiences because of his sexual energy and good looks. When producer Arthur Hopkins asked him to play the title role in Shakespeare's *Richard III* on Broadway, the actor panicked. Barrymore had neither the classical training nor the vocal range and timbre for Shakespearean iambics.

The gifted speech and voice teacher Margaret Carrington—who was the sister of Walter Huston and was married to Robert Edmond Jones—came to his rescue. Carrington's unusual methods were said to turn crows into nightingales. Unfortunately, no one today knows exactly what methods Carrington used, but she definitely emphasized breathing and rhythm. (She had an impressive singing background in England.) For weeks, Barrymore worked with Carrington five hours a day. Quickly, the papery voice took on sonority, elasticity, and precision. Consonants rapped, vowels sang, periods rang with force and authority. Barrymore called Carrington a "white witch." Inspired, he threw himself into rehearsals.

On opening night, Barrymore's strong, sonorous instrument charged the theater with electricity. Spontaneous applause burst like a fanfare, interrupting the play so many times that the first night ran until one o'clock in the morning.

"His voice is now beautifully placed, deep and sonorous and free," said the critic of the *New York Republic.* "And his body, once a rather shiftless tenement, is now a mansion, or rather a house in which there are many mansions."

In 1922, Barrymore sought out Carrington again for *Hamlet,* and this time he worked eight hours a day on voice, text, and interpretation. It was then customary for acting coaches to teach voice, speech, and interpretation as interrelated skills that served the same end. Only in recent years have these skills been taught by individual specialists and left to actors to combine.

Frances Robinson-Duff was another trainer of voices who worked with prominent American actors of the 1920s and 1930s. Producer and playwright David Belasco called her the greatest acting teacher in the world. Robinson-Duff had been a Wagnerian soprano, had acted in France, and had per-formed all over America with the best-known artists of the time. Having studied a method of breath control and voice projection with Sarah Bernhardt's teacher, she embellished, refined, and taught that method herself. Her mother was also a teacher of voice and drama in Paris, and the two women became famous for their stellar list of students. They returned to the United States at the beginning of World War I, and Robinson-Duff quickly established herself as the foremost acting and voice coach in America. Helen Hayes, Mary Pick-ford, and Clark Gable were a just few of the leading players coached by her.

With the advent of sound film, the voice was the most noticed and commented-upon element, and voice training became critical for screen actors. The great silent film star John Gilbert was said to have lost his career because of his high-pitched, feminine-sounding voice. Others say he was sabotaged by his studio. Film stars soon became known and recognized by their distinctive voices.

In New York, the young, inexperienced Katharine Hepburn sought out Robinson-Duff because she was sure the association would lead to theatrical stardom. Apparently Robinson-Duff saw something special in the neophyte, who already had a reputation for getting hired and fired in rapid succession. Hepburn worked hard with her new coach, but despite her efforts she was fired from yet another role. She took it on the chin. "Look at how I'm taking it," Hepburn told her teacher. "Not a tear! I know you're proud of me now."

"How can I ever make an actress of you, if you keep that shell over your emotions?" was the great teacher's reply. (The goals of voice teachers then were not very different from what they are today.)

Hepburn continued to work with Robinson-Duff until the teacher's death in 1951. Throughout her career, she worked with a variety of coaches. Constance Collier, whom Hepburn first met during the filming of *Stage Door,* coached her in her first Shakespearean roles. Later, she worked with Alfred Dixon, a voice and speech teacher of the time. According to Cole Lesley, Noël Coward's biographer, one of Dixon's more exotic exercises required the actor to purse his lips and moo like a cow up and down several octaves until running out of breath.

It should be pointed out that Hepburn's (and others') life-long dedication to vocal training proves that voice development never intrudes on an actor's personality. When you hear her speak, even if she is standing behind a piece of scenery, you know you are hearing Katharine Hepburn. I doubt she ever questioned whether voice training might rob her of emotional intensity or otherwise detract from her performance. She has successfully played every kind of part, from low comedy to high tragedy, and worked in every medium.

MORE RECENT DEVELOPMENTS

As in the past, innovations in acting developed in relation to new visions in playwriting. There would be no Shakespearean acting style had it not been for Shakespeare; no Stanislavski without Chekhov; and no Method without American dramatists like Clifford Odets and Tennessee Williams. Obviously, the voice had to adapt to modern changes in playwriting and staging, as did all other aspects of acting.

From the founding of the Group Theater, psychological realism dominated the American commercial theater. Impressionistic and surrealistic devices were introduced in plays by Arthur Miller and Tennessee Williams, who used memory and dream sequences and symbolic characters and language to express psychological truths.

Eventually, the stage realism associated with the Method prompted an opposite response, and Theater of the Absurd became a popular genre, influenced by developments in Europe and the theories of the French existentialist thinkers Albert Camus and Jean-Paul Sartre. In absurdist drama, there is no obvious cause and effect among incidents. Language becomes a game characters play with one another, usually to gain the upper hand, and characters are types, often grotesquely so. The result is the picture of a nonsense world occupied by alienated individuals. Two plays that expressed the absurdist view were Eugéne Ionesco's *Rhinoceros,* brilliantly performed in the United States by Zero Mostel, and Samuel Beckett's *Waiting for Godot.*

Absurdism greatly influenced American drama. Edward Albee's early plays, such as *The Zoo Story*, were classified as absurdist because of the seemingly irrational elements and actions of his characters. In England, Harold Pinter's *The Homecoming,* first produced in 1964, was also considered absurdist (Pinter himself explained that the fragments of unexplained activity and dialogue in his dark and impenetrable play make it realistic—such things simply resemble everyday life).

Later playwrights of the late 1960s and the 1970s, such as Sam Shepard and David Mamet, further explored the absurdist use of language as a game. In their plays, highly fragmentary language often sets up a barrier between characters.

TRAINING METHODS TODAY

What does our theatrical past tell us about acting today? For one thing, plays from the Greeks to Mamet and beyond are being produced today. Actors must therefore have the skills to work in all of them. Their challenges and demands are greater than at any time in history.

Almost all actor-training programs in America today involve some form of Method training in which the actor works from the inside out, identifying with a character's emotional life and using creative imagination to give the character a lifelike quality.

Whatever focus they have, all acting methods comprise a general set of rules based on what good actors tend to do anyway. Certain methods are identified with certain teachers, such as the approach developed by Sanford Meisner, but, generally, everyone is seeking the same result: reaching your goal in a professional manner, so that you don't have to wait until you feel inspired. Developing craft is hard work. Having a method gives you a way to explore and develop your talents. Different actors have different problems and, in my experience, the best usually experiment with many different methods. The English actress Wendy Hiller once described her method this way: "Well, I have a bash at it, and if it doesn't go, I have another bash at it."

Like many successful approaches, the Method developed by Strasberg and Adler has been carried to extremes, and its strongest advocates have been criticized for emphasizing inner life at the expense of total development, as if pure emotion could exist and be communicated to the audience without words and language.

Conservatory actor-training programs do include voice classes in their curricula, but often the work is not fully integrated into the actor's performance. As a result, many actors think that a few relaxation techniques, some sense memory, and rehearsals are enough to yield good acting. The truth is that acting is similar to other performing arts: If the actor's total physical and vocal instrument is insufficiently developed or flawed, all performance, no matter how large or small the role, will be diminished.

Even actors whose work seems to radiate with some inner magic often must work hard at developing their instrument. One example is the American actress Laurette Taylor, the only actor said to have had artistic powers to rival Duse's. No one understood how Taylor did what she did. In the beginning of her career, although some critics recognized her special quality, she was criticized for her weak voice. Taylor worked on her vocal instrument and worked hard. Soon the criticism was forgotten, and eventually her exquisite voice could be heard in the last row of the highest balcony.

Julie Harris is another example of an actress who was rebuked by critics for her raspy, edgy vocal quality at the beginning of her career. She, too, worked until she managed to turn her voice into a highly identifiable, rangy instrument.

On the English stage, John Gielgud mastered every aspect of movement, voice, and speech. In his book *Stage Directions,* he acknowledged his debt to the Russian director and disciple of Stanislavski, Theodore Komisarjevsky, known to his friends and colleagues as Komis. There, Gielgud succinctly put the inside/out approach in perspective when he wrote that Komis had taught him "not to act from outside, seizing on obvious effects and histrionics; to avoid the temptations of showing off; to work from within to present a character, and to absorb the atmosphere and general background of a play. . . . He also gave me my first important lesson in trying to act with relaxation—the secret of all good acting." Young actors who know Sir John from his stylish and moving film portrayals often don't realize that this supremely gifted actor, born in 1904, is one of the foremost figures in the twentieth-century theater. His Shakespearean roles were magnificent, particularly his Hamlet. Gielgud is clearly an actor who continues to study and polish his craft, and it's possible that he is even better today than when he was in his youthful prime.

Developing inner truth is the key contribution of the modern acting methods we have discussed, and today it's a given that every actor must be able to draw on what he or she personally has experienced and observed, a major element in the approach that began with Stanislavski. But great actors recognize that acting goes beyond that. Actors must know such basics of their *craft* as how to read lines clearly with meaning and emotion. They must memorize lines before building a character. Actors must be devoted to the task of creating a role, must be responsive to directors and conscientious about rehearsals, and must understand the play and the artistic ideas behind the production. If actors do not have this discipline, then the inner, emotional life is only poorly transmitted to the audience. Their own feelings remain hidden; the audience cannot see, hear, or feel them.

It should be obvious, then, that the utilizing of the inner life must be combined with outward physical and vocal technique. If actors can simultaneously come to their roles from the inside and the outside, the results are phenomenal.

The voice training you will find in this book is perfectly consistent with the American approach to actor training and is intended to be carried out at the same time. As we begin to see how, we'll consider, in the next chapter, the ideal of truthfulness in performance and explore the possibility of developing honesty in the use of your voice.

3

VOICE TRAINING, AMERICAN STYLE

I once heard Vanessa Redgrave say that observing the skill of American actors in playing psychological realism profoundly altered her view of acting. She was speaking of the American plays she had first seen in the 1950s. Most acting teachers, directors, and audiences would concur that Redgrave was referring to a quality of emotional *honesty* that she found in American acting. They would agree, too, that this is a desirable quality. Yet most would be hard-put to define what they mean by it. In terms of acting we might say that honesty is believability. In terms of vocal quality, what constitutes an honest voice? A sincere voice? A truthful voice?

An actor's instrument cannot be honest or dishonest, any more than a musician's piano or a dancer's body can. Musicians and dancers spend their lifetimes working on their instruments, and their efforts are intimately involved in the expression of their emotional lives. If they stop practicing, the artistry fails—that much is basic.

It is the same for actors. *An honest voice is one that connects the actor to his or her inner life, and thus responds to what the actor is feeling.* You must trust that your instrument will be able to do this, for the honest voice is one that is never consciously manipulated to make the audience feel a particular way. You also trust that your audience will understand that emotion.

DEVELOPING VOCAL HONESTY

Many actors equate honesty with quietness. They think the less volume and inflection they give their speeches, the more profoundly honest they will sound. Many British actors are being hired for big film roles because American directors associate their exceptional, transparent performances with quietness, a hallmark of the British style. In fact, more goes on in their performances than mere quietness. Quiet is quiet, loud is loud, and monotone is monotone. All may be honest—or not.

Honesty stems from an openness, a more revealing, uncontrived vocal quality that allows the audience to read the actor's mind and heart. American actors consider themselves emotionally honest if they avoid vocally "illustrating" and vocally "indicating" their emotion. However, the lack of the negative value does not automatically supply the positive. No matter how freely and sincerely you feel an emotion, if your physical instrument is weak, your emotion will be weakly transmitted to the audience.

The vocal flexibility and strength that you will develop through training will contribute to an honest vocal quality, yet there is more: Many actors realize that an important component of giving a fresh, interesting performance is *listening* to the other actors. Even so, few realize that listening also has a profound impact on the sound of their own voices. An actor whose voice sounds phony or self-conscious probably will not be listening to the other actors. An actor who seems to calculate pauses is probably not listening to the other actors. Likewise, an actor who speaks too loudly or too softly is not listening, for excessive loudness is distancing to fellow actors and to the audience, and excessive softness suggests that one doesn't care whether the other actors or the audience hear you at all. On the other hand, actors who really take in what the other actors are saying are much more likely to be genuinely responsive themselves.

Predetermining inflection on a particular line also tends to lead to dishonesty, and listening well is a good way to get past any preconceived ideas of how your character is supposed to sound. Your goal is to listen genuinely to the expression in the other actor's voice when he or she speaks, and for you to possess a vocal instrument which can express any emotion you feel as a result.

All the voice-training exercises in this book (see, especially, Chapter 8) are designed to help you develop an honest-sounding voice and require paying attention to resonance, breathing, and physical tension in the tongue and jaw. Unfortunately, some actors striving for naturalness in their portrayals consider this work an interference. But the conflict they suppose they will find between voice work and emotional work has been solved by modern voice training—it does not have to be a problem anymore. Voice training today involves two innovative steps to resolve the conflict between so-called technical exercises and emotions. First, the design of the workout makes the vocal instrument more supple and thus more responsive. Second, you do the exercises while you are in touch with your feelings. This does not necessarily mean you must experience profound emotion as you carry out vocal exercises, but you must feel a connection to whatever you are experiencing at the moment. As you will discover, voice exercises done in this manner lead to honesty in acting.

QUESTIONS OF APPROACH

One way or another, voice training has been, with some exceptions, part of the actor's job and a standard preoccupation of actors, audiences, and critics. Throughout the theater's history, actors have worked on their voices, sometimes using quite bizarre techniques.

As an actor, you must be very clever regarding training, ruthlessly deciding if any type of training adds to or interferes with your performances. And as I hope to show, not only the type of voice training you receive is very important, but also the timing—the point at which your training is incorporated into your acting process—is crucial.

Of the many different approaches to training the actor's voice, one fairly common one still being used by some teachers is *optimal pitch*. With this approach, the teacher determines the area within the range of the actor's voice that is best heard, and the actor learns to "place" his or her voice in that area. The problem with this method is that the actor's vocal range is being limited, and many notes in his or her voice are thus being wasted.

And more importantly, the optimal pitch method does not take into account what is being expressed. For example, if your character is calming down a hysterical child, you will want to call on the lower, relaxed part of your voice. On the other hand, if your character wants to yell, "Help!" as someone approaches with a butcher knife, you will need a vibrant, aggressive higher part of your voice. That is, the yell should happen naturally, and not be "placed" or controlled. With the optimal pitch method you will have to struggle to produce these different emotions from the same spot in your vocal range. In fact, it will be impossible. To be at your best, your entire vocal range must be available to you.

The vocal training I use is no less demanding, but it is distinctly different. We now have a greater knowledge about vocal anatomy, and as actors we also strive for different results. The approach described in this book is based on the logic of vocal anatomy—of how sound is produced in the body—and is designed for the American style of actor training in which actors strive for an honest performance using a voice that responds naturally to their emotional state. Your instrument is developed so that it *serves* your acting.

Many good examples could be found of American-trained actors whose voices have enhanced their performances, but it is instructive to consider one who was caught without a voice that could serve him in his role: Marlon Brando as Mark Antony in the 1953 film of Shakespeare's *Julius Caesar.* Brando is a wonderful actor, but his vocal instrument was underdeveloped; as a result he could not convey all of the character's internal passion. A better instrument would have made Brando even more effective and, in this case, more honest.

Part of American actors' tendency to be suspicious of voice training derives from the way we perceive our national character. Early in our history, we learned to judge people by their deeds rather than their words. American mythology emphasizes the nobility of strong, silent men and women who adhere to a code of honesty and act from inner conviction.

We admire people who live full emotional lives with considerable sensitivity, yet outwardly express little. We are, after all, a nation of doers, not clever raconteurs. When you translate the American character into an acting style (especially in the movies), you wind up with a lean, spare performance seething with underlying emotion. The audience empathizes with the actor and imagines what he or she is feeling. Good American film actors, such as Gary Cooper, have shown a remarkable ability to think and feel their roles while showing almost nothing vocally. Observations have been made time and again that if you watch good actors working in front of a camera, you can't see them doing anything. But when you see the same performance on the screen, the whole character is visible.

The English tradition more actively encourages voice development than the American. The English have a centuries-old history of valuing the spoken word and, as a natural consequence, the voice itself. Ironically, the English are now working in the American style better than we are. Alec Guinness's BBC-television portrayal of George Smiley is a masterpiece of honest, internal playing, with virtually no language or large physical expression. Anthony Hopkins's completely held-back portrayal of the butler in the film *The Remains of the Day* boils with emotion. In other words, the British are excelling at our own acting style while we fail to absorb the superior vocal technique for which they are famous.

In acting, holding back can and often does create intensity. However, we get into trouble when this leads to undervaluing the physical instrument and overvaluing the inner emotional life. Even if you take the position that emotional life is the essence of acting, that emotion must still be effectively expressed. The stronger and richer the inner emotional life, the greater the need for a superior method of release.

What we're talking about here is finding an approach that enables the actor to work at full power, using all of his or her gifts in a smoothly integrated performance. When I first started teaching in conservatory programs, voice, speech and movement were treated as separate from acting. It was assumed that training the vocal and physical instrument would somehow carry over into acting. In my first year of teaching voice in a prominent BFA program, I was shocked to learn that final scenes, performed in front of a jury of faculty members, were judged for acting alone; voice and speech were judged by poetic recitations. (Movement was not judged at all.) The faculty's view was that voices cannot be judged in the context of scenes. In their approach, no effort was made to help actors integrate voice, speech, and movement into scene work. On the contrary, much effort was spent in continuing to separate scene work from voice, speech, and movement. These acting teachers expected their students to use only the specific techniques being taught in their particular classes without any integration of other skills and knowledge.

There is no point in studying many aspects of actor training if they are not intended to be used in acting, in giving an actual performance. You cannot study different skills and expect them to magically come together. All actor-training teachers, regardless of their specialties, need to help actors integrate their skills. When skills are not integrated, performances are less than they should be; moreover, actors often wind up with vocal and acting problems. As you move through this book to the vocal exercises and then to your own work as an actor, you will discover an approach that enables you to achieve a complete range of expression as a fully integrated performer.

Heightened Awareness

A myth is often promoted about acting: It is often said that when an actor is acting well, he is so "honest" that he isn't even aware that he is onstage or before the camera. That is plain silly. The truth is, to accomplish excellent acting, you must be in a state of heightened awareness.

I sometimes hear the complaint, "I can't possibly think about my breath or my body or my voice when I am acting." My response is: "But when you are acting, can you think where the edge of the stage is? Or can you be aware of where the camera is?" Of course, you can. (And if you cannot, you aren't going to be working.)

Onstage, in addition to your body and voice, you must deal with the set and the blocking and also be aware sometimes of the stage manager and the audience. If you find the chair you're supposed to sit upon in the wrong place, you must adjust and move it or depart from the original blocking. One would hope you do not pretend that there is nothing wrong and sit down where the chair isn't. All this means that you must be super-aware, not less aware. Artists do not work in vacuums. Art—any kind of art—involves the conscious use of *craft* in order to reach people.

I do an exercise with my students that underscores this point. We rehearse a scene, and then I send them away and ask them to prepare themselves to do the scene. While they're gone, I drastically change the set. I turn the furnishings around. I remove some of the chairs, turn some of them upside down, and I move others to different parts of the stage. When the actors return, I tell them to begin. They move the chairs and do whatever they need to do to get the scene underway. Invariably, they adjust. The actor must deal with everything—all of it, all the time.

"Awareness" need not mean concern or worry. For example, if you feel your voice tightening up or going "into your throat," you should be aware of it and know what to do about it, even as you go on acting. This is the sign of a skilled professional who is aware of his or her instrument. As you do the vocal workout described in this book, you will begin to feel your voice vibrating in your body; you will become aware of your voice when you are acting and when you are simply going about the business of everyday life. You don't actually listen to yourself (a sure way to be a bad actor), but you do develop an awareness of how your instrument is working, which will allow you to make any necessary adjustments even in the midst of performance.

TRAINING THE VOICE DURING ACTOR TRAINING

I once worked with an acting teacher in a conservatory program who had spray-painted this message on the studio wall: "The Words Come Last." I know what he was driving at: Don't just repeat the words mindlessly; they must have the force of emotion behind them; they must be said by a person (or a character). However, his memorable phrase is simplistic and unworkable. What the actor ends up remembering is: "Words Don't Count" and consequently voice and speech skills don't really count. (One very respected colleague remarked to me, "What he really means is that the words never come at all." It is interesting to me that when this and similar influences became prominent in this conservatory program, the school began graduating actors with very low levels of voice, speech, and movement skills—therefore negating the point of conservatory training.) If the focus on feeling means that words and voice are not dealt with, then the instrument is not adequately addressed and the actor is never encouraged to do consistent work on developing his or her voice.

Virtually all American actor training now is based on actors using their own emotional lives. The goal is to be true, real, alive, and fresh in the part each time you do it. But how and when does voice training fit into this approach? Many actors work hard to get in touch with their emotional lives, then start thinking about developing the vocal instrument. That's like studying the emotional content of a concerto and then learning to play the piano, or exploring the emotional life and character aspects of the role of Giselle and then, at the end of the creative process, learning to dance. Voice training which is tacked on to the end of actor training will never be successfully integrated into performance.

Worse, the tack-on approach can interfere with your ability to give an honest performance. Consider the actor who spends weeks finding Hamlet's inner emotional life. In this process he doesn't use much energy. When he tries to take that Hamlet he has found onstage, his projection of much of his work is nil. He is now faced with an impossible situation. If a voice coach comes in and works with him on breathing and vocal release, his truth can and often does disappear. The great actor Lynne Fontanne explained it this way: "If you act it quietly and naturally in a small room and it sounds beautiful to you and then you go on the stage and have to project, it all seems destroyed."

Many actors know this and use it as a reason to reject voice work. Fontanne's own solution was to work with constant energy and vitality, to "act it up — fully," from the beginning, even when experimenting in early rehearsals. In that way, she said, when inner truth was realized, the voice and energy were already integrated.

With the same goal in mind, voice training takes a some-what different approach. My belief is that voice training should come before, or at the same time as, emotional and other acting work (motivation, character, and so on), and in equal measure. In this way the vocal instrument will be oper-ating fully from the beginning, so that a responsive voice can contribute to, rather than detract from, the actor's effort to develop a character's internal life and the expression of his work onstage.

4

BEING HEARD

The bottom line is that unless you are playing someone who doesn't talk, you have to be heard, one way or another. Even though many or most theatrical mediums use some form of amplification these days, every actor needs to be able to work without a microphone. Any actor who has been working for more than twenty years takes this for granted. Until the advent of rock musicals, when amplification suddenly took over the theater, stage actors assumed that their job was to be absolutely real *and* to be heard in the theater, including in the back row of the balcony. Today, many young actors mistakenly believe that they must make a choice between being real and being heard.

Of course, theaters may have good, poor, or so-so acoustics. Thus the assumption that any talented actor should be audible in any theater, expressing any kind of emotion, from the most intimate to the most powerful, is illogical and wrong. There is the added fact that if you must speak loudly in order to be heard it will change your acting; your performance cannot be the same as it is when you are intimately speaking to other actors in a rehearsal hall. Some actors have trouble accepting this fact because they have been told they should be able to make a loud sound and be intimate at the same time. They cannot. It is important to realize this.

If you are rehearsing a tender love scene in a small rehearsal studio, and then you move to a larger theater space, you will not be heard unless you speak up. Automatically your expression becomes less intimate. You have to make a decision, for you cannot just raise the volume and pretend that you are delivering the same performance. It's physically impossible, so you have to sacrifice something or, at least, change something. Your own aesthetics will enter into the choice you make. Some people prefer a strong voice, no matter what emotion is being expressed. Others dislike the larger presentation. And others prefer a more old-fashioned theatrical voice that stands out.

Most people do not go to the theater or to a film to hear a great voice. They go to see and hear a great performance. (Some, of course, think a show is good only when they're hit over the head with sound; others are willing to lean into the play and listen more closely.) As already suggested, you can develop a voice that allows you to be heard *and* that is also honest, personal, and revealing. We will discuss how developing *resonance* and other vocal qualities will help you do this. But first, let's consider three approaches to audibility that you're likely to encounter: projection, pitching up, and amplification.

PROJECTING THE VOICE

Projecting is an old-fashioned way of looking at the problem of being heard. We all use the term; it's so pervasive in the theater. But bear with me here; there are some serious drawbacks to this concept.

Ideas like "Throw your voice to the balcony," or "Remember the little old lady in the last row!" must disconnect the actor from the inner emotion. That is, exertion, or pushing sound, separates the voice from the actor's internal emotional life. The projecting "stage voice" is usually too loud, too slow, and too impersonal. With an overemphasis on articulation, it is controlled and usually includes an exaggerated, artificial speech pattern or rhythm. Because the actor's speech is manipulated into certain preplanned inflections, the stage voice becomes a distancing voice not at all useful for a contemporary actor. It is not honest, and certainly not what my voice work is all about. For instance, speak this line slowly, loudly, and with exaggerated speech (that is, with all the clichés of a "stage" voice):

> Now is the winter of our discontent
> Made glorious summer by this son of York.

It probably will sound theatrical, but it cannot possibly sound honest. Such an approach does not serve the actor's artistry.

PITCHING UP

"Pitching up" is another solution involving exertion of the voice: It simply means talking in a higher, less intimate part of the voice. Usually pitching up results in an impersonal performance and sounds elevated and "actorish." Some people like this, but, again, the voice is usually more connected to the idea of being heard, rather than being heard and being honest vocally (meaning that the voice is expressive of the actor's inner life). This voice is very limiting.

AMPLIFICATION

The best actors down through history (up to the 1950s) established an intimate, honest acting style and could usually be heard because they took it for granted that, onstage, they would be working without amplification. Actors like Maureen Stapleton, Jason Robards, and Kim Stanley were genuine and effective, although often, at the beginning of their careers, their voices were not really very intimate. Over the years their vocal quality became distinctive and their voices carried.

Broadway theaters built then were medium-sized, many with wonderful acoustics, and, even more important, audiences listened in a different way—they had learned to. Moreover, playwrights and directors deliberately allowed for a short period at the beginning of every play to let the audience adjust to listening. (You will notice this "stall" when you see an unedited revival of an older play; there seems to be a slight lapse before the central action of the play gets under way.)

Today, all working actors must deal with amplification of one kind or another at some point in their careers. No one makes a living only on small stages; you must be able to work in television and film. And a number of large theaters now rely on electronic wizardry to deliver the actors' voices to the audience. (*Victor, Victoria,* a non-rock musical, is a great example.) In very large theaters, spaces with impossible acoustics, and most outdoor spaces, there is a need for amplification.

In some cases, the existence of the sound technology has prompted the theater's architects to design a hall that can accommodate a very large audience. Actors are then equipped with body microphones ("miked"), even if they have the vocal capacity to be heard in the last row of the balcony in a normal theater. In other cases, theaters have proven to have poor *acoustics;* they are perhaps too barn-like or cavernous for the actors to be heard well and are, of necessity, "amped" to the rafters—microphones all about the stage and speakers throughout the auditorium (actors are often individually miked as well).

In these instances, miking can be a limited friend to actors, for it prevents them from having to throw their voices into a great void. However, theater people often think that amplification can overcome *any* acoustical problem. This, of course, is a mistaken assumption. *Amplification does not solve vocal problems.* On the contrary, amplification makes existing vocal problems louder and more obvious, and it also creates a host of new problems for the actor.

Amplification tends to flatten out the voice and make it less expressive. It also tends to distort the voice and separate the actor from the audience, largely because the sound emanates from a speaker that is positioned somewhere else. There is something unnatural about seeing live actors open their mouths and hearing their voices come from a place where they are not. Actors can usually hear their displaced voices coming from the speakers, also, which is distracting for the actor and distancing for the audience. (I have heard that the long-running musical *Les Miserables* is the first to use a system of amplification that does not feed back to the actors.)

The effect of amplification has gone deeper: It has also changed audiences' experience of the theater. With the help of modern amplification the audience needn't be as concentrated on the actors and what they are saying. The sound is delivered to them, rather than the audience actively taking it in. I had a student in Neil Simon's *Brighton Beach Memoirs* on Broadway who tells a story of what happened one night when the sound system failed during the first act. The actors continued playing. The audience became quieter and grew more involved in the play. Then the actors found themselves actually talking more honestly with each other. The next day the actors asked management to leave the system off. Management refused. Amplification has become the norm.

Working in Film and Television

The good actor wants to be honest onstage, in film, in every medium, which means his or her vocal approach is consistent from one medium to the other. Yet in the past twenty years I have worked with enough successful film and television actors to understand that they have certain unique vocal abilities and problems. Film actors have certain kinds of problems with amplification. One prominent film actor intentionally speaks so quietly that there is almost no vibration in his voice. I am told that he is trying to add intensity to his performance. His fellow actors often can't hear him in their scenes, which has a negative effect on their performances and his. In the sound mix, the engineer must turn up the volume on his lines so that the audience will hear him. This creates an artificial effect because the actors he was working with did not hear him during filming, and their performances are out of sync with his. All around, the final result is a less effective performance from all.

In film and television the microphone amplifies whatever is being expressed. If your voice lacks feeling, that lack will be amplified.

Film actors may tell you that paying attention to breathing comes across as phony in sound recording. They are right—if they define breathing as a mechanism disconnected from their emotions and thoughts. However, as long as your breath is linked to your thought and motivation, it helps your acting. This is particularly true when you are miked. When your breathing is connected, you cannot sound phony (see exercises 10 and 11, pages 105 to 107). The vocal workout in Chapter 8 works extraordinarily well with amplification and is designed to help actors cope with it.

As an actor you need to be aware of the advantages and limitations of being amplified. To reach full potential, you must be expressive, whether amplified or not.

DEVELOPING RESONANCE

The actor must have a well-developed vocal instrument which is able to produce sound with little physical effort. A *resonator* is an area where the voice becomes larger. (This is dealt with fully in Chapter 8.) The mask area of your face— the sinus, nose, and cheeks—is a major resonating area. There, vibrations produce an overtone in your entire voice that allows the voice to be clear and to carry more easily. American actors tend to underutilize this crucial area. When the nose and cheek area are insufficiently developed, the voice usually has a colloquial sound that seems unrefined. It works for some contemporary roles, but is inadequate for many others.

These sound vibrations are not to be confused with the sound you make by pitching up, for the overtone is present throughout most of your vocal range. It does not interfere with any expression or with the freedom of your vocal instrument. On the contrary, developing the overtone contributes to expression.

Your voice's overtone can be developed through exercises 14 and 15, which focus on the sinus and nasal resonators (see pages 111–112). When you have done this, the overtones will naturally come into the voice. Development and liberating exercises are the keys. You will be heard.

In situations where you are working without amplification,

you are going to be, let us hope, in a relatively small or well designed theater. If your vocal instrument is well developed, you will probably not have to be concerned about speaking up or projecting. Just keep on doing what you're doing. The audience will lean in a little. If a director tells you to speak up, you can do that by releasing your voice a little more. By "releasing" I mean letting go, rather than pushing or using effort. It is like the difference between dropping an object (releasing it) and throwing it. It involves opening up or expanding, rather than compensating for a weakness. Releasing the voice is addressed in all the liberating exercises in Chapter 8 (pages 113–115).

You want to make sure your release is backed up by your acting. It will be different when you speak louder, but it must remain honest. Sacrificing honesty in order to be heard is not an option.

None of this is simple. It involves taste, aesthetics, talent, and the willingness to be interested and involved in developing your vocal instrument through intelligent and effective daily workouts.

5

CHARACTER AND GENDER

Actors often ask me how to achieve a voice different from their own for a particular character role. Dustin Hoffman's voice changed, for example, when he played Willy Loman in *Death of a Salesman* on Broadway. But if you think about it, he has adopted a variety of voices during his career. Somehow he always manages to connect them to his inner feelings. However, when teachers describe "character voice work," they often mean learning how to deliver an external idea of the character's voice. In other words, you read the play and research your character, then decide intellectually what kind of voice you want to use for the part. But this is playing an idea of a voice. It is an intellectual decision, rather than a choice derived from an inner emotional experience. As such, it often rings false.

THE VOICE IN CHARACTER WORK
Many years ago, in a Broadway play about a family, the leading actress playing the mother made a conscious choice to use a nasal voice. Then the actor playing the son also decided

to make his voice nasal. Neither of these terrific actors gave a good performance because the choices were so external. That's one standard approach, but in my view it is a less effective choice.

What you want is a way to allow the voice to change through an open and responsive instrument affected by the emotional life of your character. This is a complicated issue involving acting style and personal aesthetics, and not everyone agrees on the best way to do it. I believe that character work is the same as any other aspect of an acting assignment. Creating a character, you do not want to practice making a particular sound, but rather you allow your voice to change in response to what you are expressing and experiencing. With few exceptions, the key to good character work is to develop a responsive vocal and physical instrument. Think about playing Aubrey Piper, the lead in George Kelly's *The Show-Off,* or some other boring character. You don't play him by being a boring actor. Or think of playing Laura in *The Glass Menagerie.* You cannot play this very shy character by being shy yourself. You might think that Laura's voice should be very small. However, Laura's actions and words, as supplied by the dramatist, Tennessee Williams, fully describe the nature of her shyness. What, then, does the actor supply? If she has a very expressive voice, she will be able to reveal Laura's inner life. When she talks about blue roses or her glass animals, she could be painfully vulnerable. Given the delicate symbolism of Laura's lines, it is dangerous to choose a small, weak voice. It makes more sense to use a fully expressive voice to reveal her thoughts and feelings when she does speak.

If your voice is responsive to the character's inner life and you are playing a very depressed person, your voice will probably have little energy and perhaps be deeper. If you are playing a joyful person, your voice will respond to that emotion and sound quite different. This will happen without manipulation if the instrument is open, not manipulated, and the acting is honest. People, after all, have particular voices because of certain emotional and physical realities. This being true in real life, it is also true of any character you are going to play.

When you play a character part, think about allowing your voice to respond to the character's physical reality. For example, in playing a person much older than yourself, you need to deal with the physical aspects of aging. How does aging affect the spine and the breathing? How do those changes then affect the voice? Avoid playing a vocal cliché, a particular sound that you assume an older person would have. If you approach the character from a physical point of view, and your instrument responds to the changes in the body, the result will be real.

As we have already established, you also want your voice to be affected by the character's emotional reality. Manipulating the voice to sound *as if* you are feeling something you do not really feel will scarcely ring true.

VOICE AND GENDER

Actors not only make the mistake of imposing their idea of a character's voice, they also commonly yield to cultural notions about the vocal traits of the sexes and thereby limit their vocal capability. Society imposes various vocal constraints separately on men and women. In most cultures, including our own, women are encouraged to use facial-mask resonators (nasal passages, sinuses, and cheeks), which produce clarity and brilliance, in order to seem child-like. Men, on the other hand, are encouraged to use chest resonance, which produces vocal power. As a result, both sexes are shortchanged, each using only half their vocal range, which is far too limiting if one is an actor.

Many women wind up with a breathy quality, a mixture of breath and vibration, which produces a weak, childish sound. The voice often has a simultaneously manipulating and apologetic quality. Women who dare to consciously develop chest resonance often worry that they will be accused of sounding phony and theatrical or masculine. It is seldom the case that this is a real danger. Female actors who have made the choice to cultivate the full range of their voices have told me that other people react quite positively to the change, both in their work and in their everyday lives. Other actors listening to them invariably say the female voice that includes chest resonance sounds sexy, womanly, rich, and honest, and the women themselves claim that they feel something change within themselves. When a woman's voice is stronger, she usually feels stronger.

I have gotten inquiries from female business executives who tell me that their weak voices are limiting their careers. In addition to everyday conversations with colleagues, dozens of critical career-building situations draw attention to an individual's voice. These include making client presentations, chairing conferences, and giving speeches. Executives who want to advance their careers pursue these opportunities and try to make a strong impression. A highly visible executive working her way up in the fashion industry once told me, "I'm tired of being asked to put my mother on the phone, when the caller really wants to talk to me."

Similarly, actresses tell me, "I don't want to be limited to playing ingenues or kooky parts." Just as the voice has a lot to do with cultural stereotypes, it is a factor in type casting for both men and women. Men often tell me they are expected to sound strong and invulnerable, as if they felt no emotion. Boys, encouraged to use only the lower half of their voices, wind up with little freedom to reveal what they are feeling. As a result, adult males avoid using the upper part of their voice range and, specifically, their nasal resonators. Because these habits are culturally ingrained, it is no surprise that male actors in American society are often caught in this trap.

Andy Garcia, to take one example, is an intense, captivating actor, but it's apparent that he restricts his vocal range to chest tones. Indeed, I assume he does this deliberately. Using only the lower part of his vocal range gives Garcia's voice a distinctive, almost choking sound, and gives his acting a quality of tightly controlled rage. When he loses that control in a scene, the contrast between held-in and suddenly released anger is explosive.

Garcia has clearly brought to auditions the typical masculine vocal traits that were desired. The downside of his particular technique is that much of the time the listener can't understand what Garcia is saying—the sound is buried in his chest. If he were to incorporate facial-mask overtones into his range, his voice would have more clarity without sacrificing the deep chest tones he uses to help connect himself to his emotions.

In my experience, male business executives have more trouble making vocal changes than male actors do. To many men, physical relaxation, which is needed to keep the voice flowing, feels like weakness, whereas tension feels strong and dynamic. Yet, clearly, physical tension is not the same thing as strength, and it blocks vocal production.

Relaxation is neither feminine nor masculine. Men can develop the ability to relax, which ultimately makes the male voice sound stronger and more masculine. In women, relaxation results in a warmer, richer, more womanly sound. Men sometimes need to sound more vulnerable, and women sometimes need to sound more powerful. Actors must possess all human qualities and be able to express them. It helps to understand the gender-based restrictions society has placed on you all your life and observe how these restrictions are manifested in your voice and body. Once you recognize the restrictions, you can make vocal changes.

The gender-based limitations extend to breathing. Unless they are trying to hold in their abdominal muscles for cosmetic reasons, men are allowed to be fairly free in their breathing. By contrast, women are encouraged to suck in the belly and breath only in the chest. Although few women wear corsets these days, they are supposed to look as if they do. Holding in the belly all the time is a constriction leading to tension in the whole body.

With the current popularity of aerobics classes, both men and women are walking around with held-in abdominal muscles. This almost guarantees a held-back and tight voice. I get many calls from aerobic teachers, in fact, who have lost their voices, invariably a result of constant tension in the belly; these teachers do not get enough breath to support the level of vocal production needed for teaching classes. The result is damaged vocal cords and voice loss. Many aerobics teachers now use microphones in classes, even when working in very small rooms! In doing so, they are overlooking a critical relaxation factor that could actually enhance physical training, as well as protect the voice.

To have a successful, long-lasting career, every actor, male and female, needs to develop the entire voice, bottom to top, and the capacity to be vulnerable or to be powerful. Your most moving moments as an actor will come when you drop societal constraints and show all the layers of your character's humanity. Do the vocal workout daily and explore all the areas of your voice, even those that feel awkward and foreign or wrong, masculine or feminine. Let your voice encompass all of it.

6

VOCAL POWER

Vocal power is the ability to express strong emotions using the voice. Genuine vocal power is rare. The greatest test, I believe, is one's ability to express anger: If you can be vocally powerful when expressing anger you usually can be vocally powerful in all emotional responses.

People avoid vocal power for several reasons. It can be frightening to take responsibility for what you say. When you say something with power, you clearly put yourself on the line. Vocal power means you are really saying it, and that takes courage. Because most of us have trained ourselves since childhood to be vocally subdued, developing vocal power is uncomfortable. Power feels dangerous and wrong. We've been taught that. To rationalize their habit of holding back, actors point out: "It's more intense to hold back." Actors will simply say: "Less is more." The truth is that sometimes less is simply less. Every performing artist needs the capacity to be powerful when power is called for. We all know how to hold back, if needed.

Vocally, power comes from vibration in one important resonating area of the body: the torso, or chest. You'll notice that when expressing anger many people allow their voices to go quite high in pitch, which sounds strained and—if you think about it—weak. Including chest resonance in the vocal range reduces that high squeak and produces vocal power. But adding chest resonance to your vocal range takes some getting used to. There is a distinct difference between lowering your pitch and utilizing chest resonance. The first sounds artificial and manipulated. Think about the wonderfully phony news-anchorman's voice that actor Ted Knight used on the television sitcom *The Mary Tyler Moore Show.* You could actually see Knight tuck his chin in, deliberately lower his pitch, and produce his Ted Baxter on-camera voice. From a voice teacher's point of view, his performance was brilliant. By contrast, using chest resonance sounds genuine, free, and powerful; it's full vocally.

Producing vocal power is a matter of taking a full breath, letting go, and bringing your chest resonance into play along with all your other resonators. You want to use the amount of vibration needed to match the emotion. You don't want to produce too little or too much sound for the content. If you are instrumentally open, you will naturally get the right amount of sound.

Let's say you have a role in which you must express anger. Most actors will either push their voices or hold back. If you think you express anger best by pushing, your voice probably tightens, goes higher, and sounds strident. It's possible to damage your vocal cords this way. You may think this sounds strong, but in fact, you are compensating for a constricted voice—forcing sound from a less vibratory instrument.

Moreover—and this is important—to the audience your anger thus comes across as weakness; they subconsciously pick up any residual feelings of inadequacy you have. It's often hard to stop yourself from pushing, because the physical tension created by pushing can feel like anger. When you stop pushing, you may feel you aren't expressing anything.

This is part of a strange phenomenon in acting: *When real emotion is released in the voice, the actor feels less of the emotion.* He or she lets the emotion out.

Both pushing against tension and holding back can make the actor feel more emotion inside, but the audience receives less because the actor doesn't actually let the emotion out vocally. If the actor is inwardly full of emotion the audience usually senses that something is going on within the actor, but doesn't perceive what that is. Thus, pushing or holding back never achieves the same result as actually releasing a powerful emotion.

Releasing or letting go of anger can be a real vocal challenge. For practice, I ask actors to speak the text rapidly because there is automatically more release when you're talking fast. I did this for years before I read Laurence Olivier's *Confessions of an Actor,* in which he described how he used this technique to great effect. Try it now. Speak this angry line slowly: "Now get out of here."

Now . . . get . . . out . . . of . . . here!

Now repeat the same line very quickly. If you mean it both times, the slower delivery will be more controlled. The second version will be more released.

In real life, slow delivery protects the listener from your wrath. In acting, however, you don't always want to be protective; sometimes you want to sound dangerous and threatening, or at least be powerful by being honest and open.

Here is another exercise. This is a challenging one for those who are unaccustomed to using chest resonance. It can feel dangerous and wrong to let out this kind of emotion. I change the text all the time, but it always goes something like this:

> All right, I want to deal with this now. You have made me very angry. When I tell you to do a job, I mean do it this instant. Now!

I ask my students to repeat this text in three different ways. All are honestly felt, angry, and fast, with no pauses for breath. All choices are valid, but remember when you are doing them that pushing can be vocally damaging.

1. Hold back vocally. It's honest, but held back as if you didn't want someone to hear. The expression is contained anger.

2. Push your voice slightly. I mean very slightly, so that you don't injure your voice. Use a little more effort than is actually called for, because you feel that you must compensate for a lack of something.

3. Now release the voice fully—open, honest, and with a voice that truly expresses the right amount of anger, no less, no more. Use chest resonance, without going higher in pitch. This requires a full breath.

The third exercise may seem complicated, and it may not feel comfortable. Read the directions again. It is really quite easy and invariably will increase your awareness of how you are using your voice.

As implied earlier, holding back can be a valid vocal choice—for instance, when you want to say something intense, but don't want to be heard by everybody in the next room. But you need to be conscious of what you are doing when you make that choice. Pushing is more problematic. Again, it is very possible to damage your voice when pushing.

If you are rehearsing a scene ten times a day for three days, you can get into big trouble. Remember, also, that pushing always communicates weakness. If that is your intention, then it may be all right as a choice. However, usually it is not an intelligent choice because you put yourself in a physically vulnerable position. If you push your voice in a strong scene over and over again, you can count on having some vocal problems.

If you must express hysteria, consider your own survival. In terms of physical action in performance, you cannot actually kill yourself in a hysterical fit (or another actor, unless you want to play only one performance and spend the rest of your life in jail). It's the same with the voice. You must learn, as a professional, how not to destroy yourself. With a developed instrument you will be able to be very effective emotionally and vocally without hurting yourself. Vocal power is worth working toward because it helps the actor to liberate all emotions. Including power in your range allows you to be strong when you need to be. There is something to be said for subtlety, but there is a great deal to be said for having a direct, open, powerful expression when it is needed.

7

PRACTICAL KNOWLEDGE AND DISCIPLINE

The voice workout you will learn here gives you a complete vocal conditioning regimen. The entire sequence, which takes approximately ten to fifteen minutes to perform, produces positive changes quickly. Many students are unaware of the change in their voices and discover that other people hear their improvement before they do themselves.

Among voice teachers I am unusual in saying that you may actually hear the improvement the first time you do the workout. How long it will take you to get into decent vocal shape will vary depending on your vocal status initially. Some people are satisfactory in a month, and some need as long as a year. In less than a year, actor Wesley Snipes, a gifted actor and my former student, developed a full, resonant, powerful voice (although we worked together for the full four years that he was in conservatory training).

Once they are in decent vocal shape, most actors can maintain their instruments by exercising ten minutes each day.

It's possible to use your body in a way that opens up the voice and connects it to your emotional life. With a little effort, you can change your voice into almost anything you want. An actor can almost always improve his or her voice—and fairly quickly—by applying a little practical knowledge and discipline.

I wouldn't blame you if you felt skeptical about learning voice work from the printed page. Printed exercises tend to look difficult; however, if you will give these a try, you'll feel—and hear—some change immediately. I have given my students the voice workout exercises in text form and asked them to help me revise them to make the instructions as clear as possible. If you try each exercise once, step-by-step, you will find them to be quite simple. Better than that, you will "get it" immediately. Vocal progress will come from understanding the exercises and by doing them on a regular basis.

If you are studying in an actor training program which minimizes voice and physical training, you should study on your own or seek private training. While you can do this work by yourself, you will enjoy it more if you work with a good trainer, or perhaps with another student.

PHYSICAL ASPECTS OF THE VOICE

During one legendary argument between actress Anne Bancroft and her husband, the filmmaker Mel Brooks, Brooks made a wisecrack about his wife's body. "My body!" she cried. "Don't you know my body's my instrument?"

"Oh, yeah?" Brooks said, surprised. "Then let's hear you play 'Begin the Beguine'!"

They were right on the money. Anne Bancroft's body (and mind) *is* her instrument, and my guess is that she probably has enough mastery over it to play anything she wants, including "Begin the Beguine." Actors need to know certain facts about the vocal anatomy in order to protect their instrument and maximize its potential.

Good voice work is based on an understanding of how the physical instrument works. The sound in your voice is produced by the vocal cords, just as the basic sound of a violin comes from the strings and the bow. If a violin had only strings and a bow, however, the sound would not be recognizable. Similarly, vocal cords produce only a tiny sound. Like the wooden box of a violin, your body enlarges the sound and quality of sound into what we recognize as the human voice.

As the voice changes, actors often see changes in their personalities, too. They tend to become more direct, more sensitive, and even more powerful in their presentation of themselves. As a result, they are perceived differently and more favorably by others. Actors often tell me how grounded and open they feel after doing their vocal workouts, and how much voice work has changed the auditioning and performance experience for them.

Voice training alters sound by exercising specific parts of the body that support the vocal tract. The vocal tract is a complicated anatomical feature that uses many different parts of the body to produce sound and speech. Nearly all higher vertebrates use some kind of sound as part of their coomunication system: Frogs croak, bobwhites whistle, lions roar, and crickets whisk their legs together. None owns a catalog of sounds as varied and complex as our own. Humans laugh, cry, sing, and speak, sometimes all at once.

Producing such an array of sounds requires the smooth, simultaneous cooperation of four separate anatomical systems, which together comprise the vocal tract: the throat, the vocal cords, the resonators, and the articulators. Each system is made up of several different parts.

The throat (or pharynx) begins behind the mouth and nasal cavity and leads down to the voice box (or larynx). Long muscles inside the throat constrict, helping to push food down into the esophagus; at the same time, circular muscles lift up the walls of the throat as you are swallowing. If you swallow right now you will feel both kinds of muscles working.

At the bottom of the throat is the larynx. The larynx is like a box made of cartilage. It sits at the top of the windpipe (or trachea), the passageway through which air passes. When you swallow, an elastic plate (epiglottis) in the larynx drops down to close off the windpipe. Generally speaking, a man's larynx is slightly larger than a woman's (about 1¾ inches long and about 1½ inches wide). Cartilage bulging from the framework produces the man's Adam's apple.

Inside the larynx are two small pairs of vocal cords. The upper pair are called *false* because they do not actually produce sound. The second pair are white flaps of mucous membrane; these are the true vocal cords.

As you inhale, the vocal cords naturally swing outward as air passes through. The cords remain relaxed as you exhale in the normal course of breathing. However, if you wish to speak, the voice box contracts, and the cords also contract and become rigid. The exhaled air passes over the taut cords and they vibrate, producing sound.

Vocal cords that are long and relaxed produce low-pitched sounds. The shorter and more rigid the cords, the higher the pitch. Loudness is determined by how much force you put behind your exhaled breath. The quality of your voice—its warmth, timbre, resonance, sweetness—is governed by the size and shape of natural anatomical cavities in the body. The mouth, nose, sinuses, head, neck, and chest are all cavities through which sound resonates.The resonators play a crucial part in developing the actor's voice. The fourth system of the vocal tract consists of the articulators that control speech: the lips, tongue, palate, and teeth.

The vocal workout in Chapter 8 is designed to develop and enhance the harmonious interplay of these four systems.

STRENGTHENING THE ABDOMEN

More than the vocal tract is involved in developing the actor's voice.

If you want to get in touch with your emotions and express them vocally, you need to learn to relax the muscles of your *abdomen.* It is extremely important—in order to allow freedom in breathing—to learn not to always pull in or tighten the abdominal muscles.

Still, if you intend to move around, you also need to build strength in the abdomen. For example, if you are asked to run across the stage, leap onto a high platform, and give a big emotional speech, you must first contract the abdominal muscles to make the leap; you must then release the same muscles in order to produce the emotionally connected text. For that kind of instant flexibility those muscles must be in very good shape.

In producing sound, we are mainly dealing with the diaphragm, the flat muscle separating the thoracic cavity from the abdominal cavity, and with all the muscles surrounding it: the rectos abdominus, the internal and external obliques, the transverses muscle, and the iliopsoas muscle group. When I was first trained as a voice teacher, I was taught to concentrate on the diaphragm and ignore these other muscles, as if they were "bad muscles" that shouldn't really be there. I later learned through experience that these supporting muscles are enormously useful when it comes to integrating voice and movement.

Actors should do all kinds of exercises to strengthen the abdominal muscles—crunches, sit-ups, and whatever else you find useful. Just be sure you are able to release those muscles at the end of the workout. Don't walk around all day contracting them. It's like going to a gym: You can do curls, put down the weights, and go on with your life; you don't have to contract the muscles all day.

BENEFITTING FROM CONSISTENT PRACTICE

After a month's study, a young actor once said to me, "You mean I have to do these vocal exercises again?" I was dumbfounded. Can you imagine a musician asking, "You mean I have to do this scale again?"

The only way to develop your vocal instrument is to practice. Most people are born with potentially good vocal instruments unless they suffer some physiological damage. Over time, however, people develop bad physical and vocal habits which result in an inferior instrument. It takes regular practice to reverse the process. Discipline is thus absolutely necessary for results. You don't have to practice endlessly, but you do have to do it regularly and consistently.

I always tell my students that my approach to voice work (alarming though it may sound) is much like military training. In the armed forces, one learns to follow orders instantly. Basic training is total conditioning that prepares you to respond quickly and reliably—no questions, no hesitation, no negotiation—so that in a life-or-death encounter, when you are terrified, you can do your job effectively without pulling back or falling apart.

I am not suggesting that the actor's work is anything like a soldier's, but if you consider that an actor's professional life is full of pressure and intense, often intimidating moments— during interviews, auditions, screen tests, last-minute script changes, film shoots with millions of dollars riding on them, opening nights, and so on—the comparison makes sense. You have some physical tension even when you're lying down reading a book. You have much more when you're standing up talking to people. It increases with stress, so think how much it increases when you are acting.

The actor's potential reactions to stress range from simple nervousness and stage fright to sheer terror. Potential vocal reactions include high-pitched squeakiness, a dry cracked sound, feeble production, severely restricted vocal range, and labored breathing. I've heard actors say they have nightmares in which they open their mouths to speak and no sound comes out.

If you practice releasing your voice daily, losing your voice is one thing you will probably never have to worry about. And when the stakes are raised in any situation, your vocal response will be immediate and full. This is partially due to your increased awareness. If you are conditioned properly, it is quite possible, for example, to feel nervous and still relax your neck and tongue. It is possible to be frightened out of your wits and tell yourself to breathe deeply, which allows you to feel more emotionally connected. Doing so depends on daily, effective voice work. For something as important as your vocal instrument, ten to fifteen minutes a day is not much to ask.

Why daily? Like any other skill-related exercise, effective vocal work depends on consistency. Assuming that you are doing the right exercises in the right way, consistent practice is the most important part of voice training. Vocal development is all about changing habits. You are attempting to change *very strong lifelong physical habits of bodily tension.*

Some people hold their shoulders up most of the time without realizing it. Some people walk around with the tongue pressed against the roof of the mouth. Both habits interfere with the quality of the voice. As you develop new and better habits, your instrument will also develop. But in order to maintain those physical changes, you have to continue the exercises.

It's important to remember that, for a good while, what you are used to will feel better than what is new. New techniques require much reinforcement before they begin to feel comfortable the way old habits do.

Once you have improved your vocal fitness, you should be able to maintain it by exercising ten minutes each day.

LAPSES AND OTHER PROBLEMS

The vocal workout strengthens and stretches certain muscles, which makes them more responsive and gives them greater stamina. Muscles responsible for producing sound react like any other muscles in the body: If you stop the exercises, the muscles soon return to their previous condition.

In the case of the vocal tract, you are working with relatively small and delicate muscle groups, which means it doesn't take long to effect change. I have been doing voice exercises regularly for twenty-five years. Even now, whenever I take a vacation and stop doing the exercises, I can feel my voice tighten up and change in a matter of a few days.

When this happens, people often don't recognize my voice over the phone. More importantly, I lose the feeling of vocal strength. It takes me about a week to get back in shape after one of these brief interludes. The longer you lapse, the longer it takes to get back.

It seems to me that actors fail to make permanent vocal changes for two major reasons: Resistance to change and fearing the loss of control. First, change is not always comfortable and requires some effort. That's true for all of us. Resistance to change may look like lack of discipline or laziness, but it is simply part of human nature. Yet people who are truly ambitious always find some way to overcome their internal obstacles, at least to the extent that they can take the all-important first step. Getting started leads to a feeling of achievement, which generates an even greater commitment to change. This process is natural to all of us regardless of the type of change we are trying to make: Trust that if you begin, the beneficial results will motivate you to continue and build on your success.

A more serious problem than resistance is feeling a loss of control. Actors always want to feel on top of their presentation of themselves. Voice work, however, is not about controlling the voice—it is about releasing the voice. I have heard actors say, "I don't want my voice to shake when I get emotional," or, "I feel too vulnerable and exposed when I let go." The fact is, these responses are perfectly human. Voices do shake, and at times they do sound vulnerable. You can't have it both ways: To be open and honest vocally and to be totally in control is not possible.

Let's be realistic. There are times when you will not want to do the workouts. I certainly have these times. It is easy to put aside vocal conditioning if you have no auditions, rehearsals, or performances scheduled. However, it doesn't make sense to allow your voice to get out of shape. An actor needs to be prepared and in top form at all times because he or she doesn't always know when an audition or an interview will come up. That being said, what happens if you do lay off? Don't panic. Just get started again with the regular ten-minute-a-day workout.

8

THE DAILY VOICE WORKOUT

The secret to developing an effective voice for acting is acquiring a *subtext* during the vocal workout. "Subtext," in this instance, has a double meaning. First, you must know the purpose of each exercise and recognize its effect on your instrument. If you do the vocal exercises mechanically, without thinking about why you are doing them, you will produce a voice disconnected from your thoughts and feelings. You are better off spending five minutes on your exercises while fully present and aware of what you're doing than you are spending five hours a day mechanically repeating the sounds **Huh Huh Huh.**

Second, while you carry out vocal exercises you must also be aware of your emotional life. You can't think about your shopping list and do the exercises. You can't "go blank" and do the exercises. You need to be aware of what you are feeling. That doesn't mean you have to sob or laugh your way through vocal exercises. It need not be a profound feeling—rage or joy or sadness. It can be any feeling at all, even if you can't label it.

Most of us feel several different things at once. You can train yourself to be aware of all your feelings, and you can try to express them when you are doing voice exercises. Even a simple sound like **Huh** can have emotional content. The emotion you are feeling may be unrecognizable to a listener. However, your emotions should be present, and you should be aware of them.

Having a subtext is a crucial habit of mind; it is the key to developing a free, responsive, natural voice that serves your acting in every situation. It is also the "trick" that produces effective, positive change in a minimal amount of time. In each of the exercises that follow I will show you how to use subtext.

These exercises are fairly simple to carry out, but the underpinnings of each is very sophisticated, based on specific anatomical realities. The purpose of these exercises is to relax the vocal instrument while maintaining focus and energy, which is an ideal state in which to act a role.

The principle of exercise is to teach you to recognize tension in a given portion of the vocal anatomy and to train your muscles to respond to the message "Release." It's hard to believe that voice training is so simple, but I've seen it work thousands of times.

TIME AND PLACE

Do your daily workout where and when it works best for you. Try to choose a place where the strange and sometimes loud sounds you will be making don't inhibit you. Remember, it's only for ten minutes.

The advantage of doing the workout in the morning is that your voice will be warmed up for the rest of the day. If you prefer to do it at night, it's better to do it then than not at all.

If you're currently working in a show or auditioning often, use the workout as your warmup. Running through the workout immediately before you audition, rehearse, or perform warms up your vocal instrument and also warms up your instincts, putting you in a good frame of mind for performance. Pre-performance voice exercises are also a good antidote to that horrible feeling of simply throwing yourself into the void. Knowing how to make your work effective is better than praying, "May the gods be with me tonight!"

Some actors do both a complete morning warmup and then a quick version before their show.

SEQUENCE OF EXERCISES

The workout consists of a sequence of exercises, and it's important to perform the exercises in their proper sequence. The sequence provides a natural warmup and builds to more muscular exercises, and it connects the breath to your emotion, increases vocal resonance, and finally frees the voice. The sequence is designed to give you maximum effect in a minimum amount of time.

As a general rule, you should repeat each exercise until the desired effect is accomplished. That is, if the exercise is designed to release neck tension, repeat it until your tension is eliminated. Sometimes you may not have enough time to get the maximum effect. This is especially true in the beginning, when you are unfamiliar with the exercise and it takes longer to successfully complete each one. But, ideally, that's what you are aiming for.

Below, I introduce you to each exercise. As you read the full description, "walk through" the exercise with me, right where you're sitting. Following that are condensed versions of the same exercises that will serve as your "coach" in the weeks that follow. Each day, you can use the capsule descriptions for your vocal workout. If you find you need more detail, come back to this chapter and reread the full description. In a few weeks, each exercise will feel familiar to you.

Finally, the Appendix provides a simple list of the exercises in their proper sequence. After you are thoroughly familiar with the exercises, you can use the list as a daily reminder. Soon, the sequence will be firmly embedded in your memory, and you will be able to run through the workout without referring to the text at all.

BODY ALIGNMENT

The exercises in the workout are designed to relax the major muscles that support the vocal instrument. Relaxing major muscles prevents straining of the smaller muscles in the throat and face.

The first two exercises will teach you to release the back of your neck, one of the major problem areas in vocal production, and the spine and belly. These are the three most important areas of the body for voice production.

1. Neck Release

Imagine that your head is held up by a string attached to the ceiling. You cut the string, and let your head fall forward. Try it now, and then bring your head back up.

Often the best way to recognize relaxation, or release, is to compare the relaxed state to its tensed counterpart. So now imagine that you are very carefully moving your head forward. You are controlling it, letting your head go forward in a very careful movement. Think about the difference in the quality of the two neck movements: The first time you just let your head drop and you did not control it. The second time, you were carefully controlling the motion of your head.

To release the back of your neck, you want to practice the first version. Try it a few times now. Again, imagine that a string attached to the ceiling is holding up your head. Cut the string, and let your head drop forward. Feel the release in the back of your neck.

That's the whole exercise. Try it a few times. Cut the string, hold your head up, let the head drop forward. Feel the release of the muscles.

2. Curling Over

The second exercise continues from the first.

Drop your head forward, as above. Begin to curl over, letting your shoulders and chest roll over, your arms dangling in front of you. Let your knees bend, and roll down, continuing to drop your head and shoulders forward. When your hands almost reach the floor, let go. Let your hands brush the floor, and simply release all your tension and dangle. Let your head bob.

Once you're all the way down and fully released, lift your head up. Now release it again and let your head bob.

Now, with your neck released, start to come back up; start at the base of your spine. In a rolling motion, come all the way back up, bringing your head up last.

The point of this exercise is to release the spine, abdomen, and stomach muscles, and to learn to recognize the difference between a tense neck and a released neck.

Try it again. Drop your head forward; roll downward, rounding your spine, your knees a little bit bent. At the bottom of the bend, just let go. Now lift your head up and drop it. You should feel the release in the back of the neck.

If you don't feel the release, lift your head up again and let it go. Do it a couple of times.

Then start to roll back upward, letting your head come up last. Don't suck in your belly coming up. This is not an aerobics exercise. Just let your belly hang out there.

Keep your knees bent while going down and while coming up, until you are all the way up. Finish in a fully erect posture. Your body will be completely relaxed, and your spine and neck will be in alignment.

THE VOCAL PASSAGEWAY

The vocal passageway comprises the throat, the back of the tongue, the soft palate (the top of the throat), the front of the tongue, the jaw, and the neck. Seven exercises concentrate on stretching the muscles in this critical voice production area. These are important exercises that directly affect the sound of your voice.

3. Tongue Exercise

When you hear people say an actor's voice is "in his throat," what they are really talking about is the tongue being tense. Emotional stress makes the tongue tense up. If you've ever lost your voice, or found your voice going very high or otherwise changing dramatically when you're emotional, it's usually the tongue that is tensing up. This is caused by old conditioning that stems from childhood. When we were children we learned our good manners, to be civil, and not to scream or screech. Most of us instinctively found that the best way to hold back emotions is to tense the bottom of the tongue. By the time you'd become an adult, the tension felt completely natural. But it doesn't work for actors who have a desire at times to be vocally and emotionally open.

You learn to release this muscle by stretching it. This requires a particular movement that must be done correctly to avoid damage to the jaw joint. Be very careful with this exercise, and follow the directions precisely.

Relax your jaw. Take one hand and gently push your jaw down and back. It's basically a diagonal movement backward. (Do **not** go forward; you can take the jaw out of its hinge.) If you wish, you can hold your jaw with your hand all the time you are doing the exercise.

Having pushed the jaw down and back, now smile with your upper lips. Lift up the muscles to create a big phony smile. Put the tip of your tongue behind the lower teeth and try to stretch the middle of the tongue out to the sides.

With the tip of the tongue still behind the lower teeth, relax the middle of your tongue. Keep your hand on your jaw; do not let your jaw come forward.

Another, stronger version of the same exercise is to lift your head up and look toward the ceiling. As your jaw goes back and down, push it back with your hand. Put the tip of the tongue behind the lower teeth; stretch the middle out, and let it go back.

By stretching your tongue like this, you are actually elongating and stretching your throat.

4. Big Yawn

This is actually a stretching exercise for the soft palate, which is the top of your throat, including the little moveable part in the back of your mouth where the uvula quite visibly hangs down. The soft palate is responsible for the overtone in the upper and middle resonators, or what is called the mask area around the nose and the sinuses. Think of the overtone as like a buzzing that helps your voice to carry and sound clear. Developing the overtone is very important to every actor, particularly for clarity and carrying power.

The soft palate has to be flexible, responsive, and able to work on its own. But it is not a part of your vocal instrument that you want to use consciously when you are speaking. If you open it up consciously you will sound unnatural—a bit like Kermit the Frog on *Sesame Street*.

The soft palate moves up and down. To stretch it, all you have to do is yawn. (Make sure your jaw doesn't come forward.) You can yawn with your mouth open or closed. The yawn stretches the top of your throat. Actually, the stretch is a little stronger with the mouth closed, which is done as if you were trying to stifle a yawn.

Exercise both the tongue and the soft palate on a daily basis, and then forget them and let them work on their own. Don't manipulate them when you speak. Remember the weight-lifting example: You pick up the weights and do the exercises, then put them down; you don't carry them around all day with you. It's the same with the tongue and soft palate. Exercise them and then forget about them. Let them do their jobs.

5. Whispered Keh

The purpose of this exercise is to increase the muscularity of the soft palate and back of the tongue so that they will quickly and naturally respond to your impulse to speak.

Breathe out on a **Keh** sound. Now, put soft palate and tongue together, as you would pronouncing the **Ng** sound in "Ri**ng**." Breathe in on the **Keh**.

Alternate the two sounds—breathing out and breathing in on the **Keh**. You are using no voice here, only the soft palate and the tongue. It's out on a **Keh**, in on a **Keh**.

This may take some experimentation. Once you feel comfortable doing it out and in, do two out, two in: Two **Keh**s out, two **Keh**s in.

If it seems difficult to breathe in on a **Keh** sound, try this: Put the soft palate and the tongue together, as if you are going to breath out on the **Keh**; keep it there, lift the soft palate up and the tongue down, and let air come in. It will feel awkward, but keep playing with it and you will get it.

6. Ngah Ngah Sound

This is another exercise to build flexibility into the soft palate and the back of the tongue. Make an **Ng** sound, as at the end of the word "Ring". Then make an **ah** sound. Now combine them: **Ng-ah**.

On the **Ng** sound, you're bringing the soft palate together with the tongue, and on the **ah** sound you are separating them. Do this two times: **Ngah Ngah**.

Continue to repeat the two.

You can do it on slightly different pitches. Without straining, play with different notes and different parts of your voice, but in a comfortable part of your voice. With the exercise you're waking up the muscles, getting them to respond and then to release.

To make the exercise even more effective, relax your tongue and put it out on your lower lip. Make the sounds **Ngah** twice, with your tongue staying on your lower lip. You can hold it there if you choose. This is like adding weights to the barbell, making the exercise more difficult and more effective.

7. Tongue Relaxer

This is a simple, very effective exercise to relax the tongue, which will add clarity to your sound. You are dealing with the whole tongue, from the very back to the very tip. A relaxed tongue will feel heavier, probably thicker, and maybe even too big for the mouth. That's only because you are used to keeping it tense.

Put the tip of your tongue on your lower lip and think about relaxing your tongue. Without forming a word, let out a sound, like **Huh**. Let the sound come out without doing anything to your tongue. Don't let it pull back or tense up. Just let the tongue stay on your lower lip. It will feel awkward because you're not used to it.

Let the **Huh** sound come out. It's easier if you let a little air come out before the sound starts. When you let out just a bit of air, an exaggerated aspirant, an "H" sound, comes out after it. Keep your tongue lying on the lower lip.

Repeat the exercise using different vocal pitches. These should be easily voiced pitches, without straining. Put the tip of your tongue on your lower lip, be very conscious about relaxing it, let out a little air, and make an unformed **Huh** sound. Let the sound be whatever feels comfortable in your voice. Practice keeping the tongue really relaxed.

As you do this exercise, you will feel your tongue becoming thicker and heavier. The sound you make during the exercise is a very weak sound, but the end result is a fuller speaking voice. But take note that the change you hear may be only subtle at first.

The most important part of this exercise is to be conscious of what you're trying to do. You have to think about relaxing your tongue even as you do it.

8. Jaw I: Relaxation

You see actors in film closeups with jaw tension all the time: the teeth-clenching, jaw-flexing Clint Eastwood school of acting. When tension is held in the jaw, the voice is constricted and so is expression.

The secret of keeping the jaw relaxed while speaking is to relax the back of the neck. The back of the neck is a very defended area of the body. It is often tense, which shortens the neck muscles. If you can relax your neck, your jaw will automatically be relaxed.

Take one hand and gently move your jaw back and forth diagonally, a down-and-back movement—not strictly up and down. You're basically testing to see if the jaw muscles are released and encouraging them to release further. Continue to move your jaw back and forth very easily, and think about releasing the back of your neck.

When your jaw and neck begin to feel loose, try making a simple **Huh** sound while you're doing it.

Try using different pitches for this sound as you continue to move your jaw, keeping the back of your neck relaxed.

This can be a frustrating exercise for people with extremely tight jaws. Some people find that when they try to move the jaw it clenches even further. Stay with it and gently persevere. It takes time, but at some point you will be able to move your jaw fluidly back and forth.

Some people find it easier to do this exercise while lying down. You might try that and see if it helps you. (If you are lying down, the muscles in back of the neck should feel very released, because no muscles are being used to hold the head up.) With your knees up and your feet flat on the floor, lie in a comfortable position. Gently move the jaw back and forth.

Remember, you can never force a release. All you can do is coax yourself and send a message by thinking: "Relax the jaw, relax the back of the neck." It may take several weeks before you actually notice a result and hear a more open quality in your voice.

Some people clench their jaws while they sleep, which means the jaw is going to be tense when they wake up. If this sounds like you, do this jaw exercise when you get up in the morning. Very occasionally people also have problems with poor jaw alignment, which requires help from a dentist.

Continue practicing this exercise and you will be able to effect a change.

9. Jaw II: Isometric

This is an isometric exercise that can help relax a very tight jaw. In isometrics, two parts of the body push against each other with equal force, so that neither one moves.

It's *very* important to do this exercise correctly or you can damage the jaw joint. The exercise is in five steps:

- Put your left fist against your left cheek, right next to your mouth. Push your fist toward your cheek into the jawbone and push your cheek toward your fist. Neither one should move. Hold it for about seven seconds, and release.

- Repeat the exercise on the other side—the right fist against your right cheek. Push toward your jawbone, with no movement. Hold it for seven seconds, and release.

- Grasp your chin with your hand and push down; push up with your chin at the same time. Hold it for seven seconds, and release.

- Put your fist underneath your jaw, at the chin. Push up with your fist; and push down with your jaw. Hold it for seven seconds, and release.

- End the sequence by moving your jaw back and forth.

CONNECTING VOICE TO BREATH

There are only two ways that human beings can produce sound: You can produce your voice with muscular tension, or you can connect your voice to your breathing and let your breath produce the sound. We have discussed why sound carried on the breath is by far the most useful for an actor's voice. These are the exercises that help you feel the connection between your breath and your voice.

10. Centering

Lie on the floor on your back, keeping your knees bent. Place one hand on your lower abdomen, or belly. Try to release those muscles; let go of any tension in them. Your breath will seem to drop down into your abdomen. In reality, the diaphragm is freed because you're not holding in your belly. (The breath, of course, does not really enter your stomach.)

Now employ an image: Think of your breath going into your lower belly—you're just letting it go in there. While you're lying on the floor, you're not making any intense physical exertion, so you need very little breath. You want the breath to go down into the belly and then just let it come out, just as you do when you're sleeping. Don't control it or sustain it. You want to let go. You are relaxing the muscles, allowing the breath to go into your belly and letting it leave without controlling it.

One of the usual mistakes is pushing the breath out. You don't need to do that. Another common mistake is holding your breath, so that you do a kind of slow, controlled breathing, perhaps counting while you breathe in and out. That's not what you are aiming for here. You just want to let it flow in, and then let it leave without any control.

Next, sit up on the floor and cross your legs in whatever sitting position feels comfortable. Place one hand on your lower belly and see if you can let the breath drop into the belly and then escape. Work with it until you feel some progress. It may take five minutes or more before you can actually release those muscles.

After you've done the exercise in a sitting position, try doing it standing up. Keeping your knees relaxed, put a hand on your lower belly and see if you can release the muscles and let the breath in easily.

Many people, especially women, feel that when they release their abdominal muscles their belly becomes much larger, almost as if they were pregnant. You should know that although the belly feels enormous, in reality the visible change is minimal. It feels big, but it does not look like you are slouching or suddenly developing a pot belly.

While you're doing the breathing exercise, let yourself tune into whatever you're feeling. It doesn't have to be anything profound. Just acknowledge the feeling, even if you can't label it, and let the breath go in and easily come out. There's a point to this: To train the voice to be connected to your emotional life. The key to having your voice be emotionally revealing is breathing freely while you are in touch with your emotional life. Without awareness of your emotional state, your voice will be disconnected, placed, and manipulated. It's simple once you get the hang of it.

11. Sound Vibration

Now think of this image: Your sound actually comes from deep down inside your belly (we know this isn't true, of course; sound comes from your vocal cords). Employ the image that the sound is coming from deep down in your body. You can picture it, and it will be an effective way to get the voice connected and supported by the breath. Basically, you are working with two images: first, that the breath is going down into your belly, and second, that the sound is also coming from down there. As you work with those images, you will make a connection between your voice and your breath.

Pretending for the moment that your voice is coming from your belly—that it's deep down inside—let out a little unformed sound, something like **Huh**. Just imagine that tiny **Huh** sound coming from your belly. Also produce that sound using a couple of other vocal pitches, without straining. You can place your hand on your belly, if you'd like.

You are putting things together at this point: breathing without manipulating the breath, without any pushing or any controlling; imagining that the sound of your voice is coming from deep inside your belly; working with an image, even if part of your brain is saying "This isn't right." Play around with easy pitches on the **Huh** sound, and see if you can feel the connection between your breath and your voice.

After you have gained some practice, combine this exercise with Exercise 2, Curling Over: While playing with the sound **Huh** on different easy pitches, drop your head forward and, with a rolling motion along your spine, bend all the way over. Let go when you bottom out, exaggerating the release of tension; then pick your head up and release it again. With your head bobbing, feel the release in the back of your neck. Then, with your neck and belly muscles released, "roll" back up, all the time continuing to produce the **Huh** sound employing different pitches.

In your daily workout, do this exercise in all three positions—first lying down, then sitting up, and finally standing up. Doing the combinations introduces you to the feeling of producing sound from a relaxed instrument. This is a natural process that you want to carry over into your everyday life. It will take some time and some practice, but you will be able to apply it to your work.

With these exercises you're training your body not to interfere with the natural process of producing sound on the breath. Eventually, the body will recognize that this is a more efficient way of expressing sound and will welcome the change.

THE RESONATING CHAMBERS

Your whole body is a resonator. The vocal cords are like the strings of the violin, and your body is like the hollow wooden case. Violin strings and vocal cords make only a very tiny sound by themselves. The sound is increased as it resonates through the body. The whole body actually vibrates. If you are aware of it, you can sometimes feel sound vibrating all the way down to the tips of your toes. We have seen how certain key areas, called resonating chambers, are known to increase sound: The chest, for example, has its most dramatic effect on the lower parts of your vocal range; the hard palate and the sinus area affect the middle range and enable your voice to carry; and the top of your skull, the highest resonator, helps you produce the highest part of your range.

Together, these major resonators contribute to the full range of your voice. If you use only some, and not others, your range will be limited. If you use all, but they are weakly developed, your range will be weak.

But if you practice sending sound to the resonating chambers, starting with your chest and going all the way up to your skull, your range will be fluid and connected. In this way you're covering all the areas of your voice and, with time, each will become fully developed.

In the next group of exercises, we're going to practice producing sound from these resonators. The amount of vibration you will get in various resonators depends on how relaxed the body is, how toned the muscles are, and whether you are comfortable sending sound to that particular area.

For example, women often avoid producing sound through the chest resonator in an effort to sound more feminine or more socially acceptable. Men tend to avoid using the upper resonators because they fear showing vulnerability. Thus, they try to hold their voices down in the chest area where it feels stronger. Actors, men and women, need to become comfortable sending sound through all of the body's major resonators so that they have a complete instrument to communicate with.

12. The Chest

The chest is the power source of your voice, supplying the entire bottom half of your range. This is a very large resonator, and you can often get much more from it than you're accustomed to using.

Lift your head up just a little bit, a couple of inches. Let your mouth drop open, as if you'd gone to asleep. Just let it fall open. Make an **Aahhh** sound—a sigh, with a downward inflection, going through the chest area. Let a little bit of air come out first, before you produce the sound; this will help keep your tongue relaxed. A little bit of air, then a sigh—and make it a very long sigh: **Aaaaahhhhhhhh.**

Place your hand on your chest and feel the vibrations. This is the lower part of your voice. The lower the resonator, the lower your pitch. The low sound you are working with right now is going down into your chest. So, make a downward inflection on the **Aahhh,** and let the sound go into your chest.

Now lift your arms above your head and let them drop— just let them go. Try to let your voice drop just as you did with your arms. Just let it go, dropping that sound out of your throat and down into your chest.

13. The Hard Palate

The hard palate, the roof of your mouth, is a round, hard surface in front of the soft palate. The soft palate moves, and the hard palate does not. The hard palate is an important resonator for your voice, but how can you exercise it?

Put your finger in your mouth, but without touching anything, and blow air on your finger. Feel the breath touch your finger. Now, send a **Huh** sound onto your finger. Do you feel a vibration?

The hard palate is a very small resonator compared to the chest, so it may take a couple of weeks of repeating this exercise before you become sensitive to the vibration. But the sound is vibrating even if you can't actually feel it yet.

Continue to do the exercise, sending a **Huh** sound onto your finger. Eventually, you will be able to feel the sound on your finger. Now continue the exercise without putting your finger in your mouth; just send the **Huh** to the front of the roof of your mouth, and let it come out. Basically, you're placing the sound in this tiny little area of your voice. When I do this exercise I feel the effect more in the front half of my mouth, rather than in the back.

Because the hard palate is a higher resonating area, your pitch is also higher. Play around with the two different sounds you produced in the hard palate resonator and in the chest resonator (exercise 12, above). Go from one to the other, and feel the difference in pitch and in where the sound is vibrating in your body.

14. The Sinuses

The sinus resonators are on either side of your nose. If you put two fingers right next to your nostrils, you will feel that the flesh there is soft. That's the resonating area we are talking about. This exercise will increase the blood circulation to the tissue in that area, which in turn will drain the sinuses. When the sinus cavities are well drained, vibration increases and your voice carries better.

You can use various sounds for this exercise, but let's stick with the simple, unformed **Huh** sound. You're going to do this on different pitches. Again, because the sinus resonators are even higher in your body, the pitches will be higher than in the previous exercises.

On different pitches, send the sound **Huh** out of your mouth (not through your nose). Put two fingers alongside each of your nostrils and massage the sinuses as you do different pitches. Just gently move your fingers up and down.

Go up a scale with easy notes. Go higher than the pitch you used when vibrating the roof of your mouth. All the while, massage the area on either side of your nostrils. You won't feel a lot of vibration while you do this; you will mainly feel the pressure of your fingers. But after you finish you may hear more resonance coming from that area when you speak.

This is tricky. You only consciously use the sinus resonator while doing the exercise. When you are actually speaking, you do not ever want to isolate sound in this area. The purpose of the exercise is to help the sinuses drain, which helps keep the sinus cavities hollow, which in turn gives your speaking voice more resonance and clarity.

15. The Nose

The nasal resonator, together with the sinus resonator (which you worked on in the previous exercise) is called the *vocal mask*. These two resonators are responsible for a vocal overtone throughout your entire range that gives the voice clarity, brilliance, and carrying power. It's a kind of buzzing in your voice.

Wrinkle up your nose and send a **Ne-Ne-Ne** sound right into the nose: **Ne-Ne-Ne**. I know, it's a very strange sound, an aggressive, strident one. Do it anyway: **Ne-Ne-Ne**, right through the nose. You can do it on various pitches.

You will probably feel some tightening in your throat, so be careful not to overdo the exercise. Your goal is to produce the high-pitched **Ne-Ne-Ne** sound while your neck and tongue are completely relaxed. Slowly moving your head from side to side as you do the exercise will help coax the back of the neck to relax.

You can also do the exercise with your tongue out on your lower lip in a relaxed, loose, soft manner.

You want the **Ne-Ne-Ne** sound to be in your nose, not in your throat. You will probably go through a phase where the sound is half in your nose and half in your throat. If you continue to do the exercise while consciously relaxing your neck and tongue, eventually you will be able to do it through your nose. Practice this exercise only a few minutes at a time.

16. The Skull

The last major resonating chamber is the skull, which you can think of as the very top of your voice. Voice work in this area will strengthen the entire voice and extend your upper range. For men, using this upper resonator produces a very distinct sound, the *falsetto*. Female singers call this their "head voice," but I discourage you from thinking of the voice in this way. I find that singing terms such as "head voice" and "chest voice" are limiting for actors. I would prefer that you think of different resonating chambers, all connected.

In this exercise, you want to send a high, long **EEEE** sound, on different pitches, up into your highest resonator. Bear in mind that the higher the pitch, often the greater the tension in your body. One excellent way to prevent your body from tensing up during the exercise is to curl over (as in exercise 2), rolling down the spine, while you're doing it. So drop your head forward, roll down your spine, curl all the way over and let go at the bottom of the curl. Allow your head to bob and your neck to be absolutely free.

Now, create the **EEEE** sound while you are dangling in that position. If you do the **EEEE** exercise from this fully relaxed position you will not have to physically reach for the notes. Stay down for a minute or two, then curl back up along the spine.

Liberating Your Voice

In the previous group of exercises, you practiced sending sound to specific resonators of your body. In this final group you will let the sound go wherever it wants to go. You are going to practice using your body in a way that completely opens up the voice.

17. Knees Only

Try this: Begin standing relaxed. Bend your knees a bit, and then straighten them again. As you bounce a little this way, going gently up and down, let out a very easy **Hah** sound as you bounce. If your body is very relaxed, your voice will also bounce up and down. In other words, your voice will be affected by the movement of your body. Your voice will shake. This is the kind of connection you want to make when you liberate your voice.

18. Larger Movement I

Very easily, move your knees up and down, bending your legs a little bit and then straightening them. Or jump up and down very gently. Say this line: "My name is (*your name*)."

Let your voice respond to the physical movement. Let it shake and let it stand still.

Now try it again, but this time while you gently bounce up and down, do whatever you can to prevent your voice from shaking. That is exactly what you want *not* to happen, but it will be useful to feel it done "wrong."

Tighten your neck, or tighten your belly. Sometimes you can stop your voice from shaking if you speak very quickly or use it very lightly. Stopping your voice from shaking while you are moving requires some kind of tension and holding, and any method you use will disengage your voice from your body.

Again, this is the opposite of what you want to happen, and you will feel the difference. Your goal is to liberate your voice, so that it does shake when you are moving. That is when you will get the most released voice possible. When you bounce up and down, your voice should shake. That is the correct form.

19. Larger Movement II

While you are gently jumping up and down, letting your voice shake, very easily make a **Hah** sound with a downward inflection, and let the sigh run from the very top of your range all the way down through the bottom. Your goal is to let your voice respond freely to the physical movement of your body. Make the **Hah** sound accompanied by the physical movement. This is how you learn to produce sound in a liberated way.

Next, repeat the same downward sigh, from the top of your range to the bottom, but do this while standing still. This should give you a sense of how it feels to use your real voice—the free voice that would shake if you were jumping.

Finally, do it jumping again, and allow the voice to shake through all the resonators.

The way to discover your real voice is to practice making any sound while jumping and letting your voice shake. If you practice using a sentence, you will have to slow it down a little bit. (You cannot do this exercise fast.)

Once again, stand still, and repeat **Hah Hah Hah**. Your voice doesn't shake, but you stay connected.

20. Finale

The final exercise in the sequence lets you end the session performance-ready. You are going to take any piece of material—a speech, a sentence, a poem, whatever you wish—and free it up while you are doing a loose physical movement, which means that your voice will shake. You can bounce up and down, fling yourself around in a swirl, or roll around on the floor. Do any physical movement that feels loose.

Try to act the speech *while* you liberate your body. You will probably feel very silly, but this exercise is the critical step for you to feel your voice coming out while it is fully connected to your body.

Try alternating between physically freeing your body while saying a line of dialogue, and then standing still while saying the same line, using your voice in the same way.

If you have trouble making the connection while you are standing still, try this: Move on the first couple of words, then stop moving and let the voice continue to come out. That way you can train yourself to use the same connected, free vocal production when you are still.

SUMMING UP THE WORKOUT

The sequence of the vocal workout takes you from relaxing the muscles of your body, to connecting your voice to the breath, and toning the vocal resonating chambers. It ends by liberating your voice. By the time you have finished the sequence, you are in full acting mode and are ready to begin. This is the workout I want you to do every day.

The secret is this: If you do the workout routinely every day you will develop a very fine vocal quality. Good vocal quality is a small goal for an actor. You want much more than that.

You want your voice to be open and honest and to serve your acting.

Never do your voice workout by "spacing out" mentally and simply repeating the exercise by rote. You have to know what you're doing and why. You have to be in touch with yourself.

If you work out with purpose and intent you will get maximum results in minimum time. Your sound will become more developed, your range extended, and your voice more open, more expressive, and more revealing.

A CAPSULE VERSION OF THE DAILY WORKOUT

Once you have accustomed yourself to the daily workout, this concisely worded version will come in handy as guide. An even briefer version—really just a reminder list—follows this version for quick reference.

Body Alignment

1. Neck Release

Drop your head forward. Do not control the movement. Just let it go.

Repeat until you feel relaxed.

2. Curling Over

Let your head drop forward. Allow your torso to roll down toward your feet, letting go at the bottom. Dangle.

Roll back up to a relaxed standing position.

Do not hold the belly.

Allow the knees to release; bend a little bit.

Make sure there are two releases—the head at the start, the neck when you reach the bottom. The head should bob.

Repeat three or four times.

The Vocal Passageway

3. Tongue Exercises

Place the tip of your tongue behind the lower teeth.

Release your jaw backward (not forward).

Roll the middle of the tongue forward, keeping the tip behind the lower teeth.

Do not allow the jaw to go forward. Hold it with your hand.

Try turning your face up towards the ceiling.

Repeat several times.

4. Big Yawn (Soft Palate)

Let your jaw go back toward the back of your neck.

Yawn or stifle a yawn, letting the soft palate rise. Do not allow the jaw to go forward, but only backward toward the back of your neck.

Repeat several times.

5. Whispered Keh

Breathe in and out on a whispered **Keh** sound.

Make sure that the soft palate and back of the tongue come together on the outgoing and incoming breath. Make sure the jaw is not moving. Put one finger on the jaw to hold it still.

Use only the soft palate and the back of the tongue to produce the **Keh** sound.

Repeat about twenty times.

6. Ngah Ngah Sound

The soft palate and the back of the tongue come together, as you make an **Ng** sound, followed by an **ah** sound: **Ngah**.

The jaw should not move. Put a finger on the jaw to hold it still. Only move the soft palate and the back of the tongue.

Repeat about twenty times.

7. Tongue Relaxer

Put your tongue out on your lower lip. Keep the tongue relaxed, and produce a **Huh** sound.

Let a little air come first, before the sound. Repeat about twenty times, on different pitches.

8. Jaw I (Relaxation)

Very easily move the lower jaw back and forth toward the back of your neck.

Make sure your neck is relaxed. If your neck is relaxed, it will help the jaw relax.

Repeat about twenty times.

9. Jaw II (Isometric)

Hold your fist against your jaw in four positions: on the right and the left sides, then pushing down and pushing up.

Do not allow your jaw to move. Keep it aligned.

CONNECTING VOICE TO BREATH

10. Centering

Lie on the floor on your back. Relax your abdominal muscles and let the breath go down into your belly—as low as possible.

Let it come out again. Do not manipulate your muscles.

Continue to allow your breath to go in and out of your abdomen, as if you were sleeping.

Do the breathing exercise also while sitting up; then do it standing. Remain in each position until you feel comfortable.

11. Sound Vibration

Pretend that the sound comes from the abdomen. Allow a **Huh** sound to come out from your belly.

You are not using articulators. Imagine that the sound is just a very plain, unformed sound coming from your belly.

Using different pitches, repeat about twenty times.

THE RESONATING CHAMBERS

12. The Chest

Use an **Ah** sound. Allow the **Aahhh** to sigh in your chest.

Lift your head slightly. Your throat is relaxed. The back of your tongue is relaxed. Your neck is relaxed.

Repeat about ten times.

13. Hard Palate

Open your mouth. Send **Huh** into the roof of your mouth. The pitch should be higher than a chest resonator. Put your finger in your open mouth and send a breath on to it. Then send a sound on to your finger.

Repeat about ten times.

14. The Sinuses

Put two fingers on either side of your nostrils and massage that area.

Simultaneously, let our the same **Huh** sound as before.

Go up and down a scale, as you continue to massage the area. Let the sound come out of your mouth.

Keep your tongue, jaw, and neck as relaxed as possible.

Repeat on eight to ten different notes.

15. The Nose

Send a **Ne-Ne-Ne-Ne** sound right into the nose. The sound should come out of your nose, not your mouth.

Let the sound spread across your face.

Lift your cheeks up. Keep the back of your neck relaxed.

Repeat about six times.

16. The Skull

This is the very top of your voice. Use an **EEEE** sound and send it to the very top of your range. Try to keep your jaw released. (You can move your jaw back and forth as you send the sound.) Keep your neck released.

Repeat eight to ten times.

LIBERATING THE VOICE

17. Knees Only

With your feet on the floor, knees bent, bounce gently up and down, saying **Hah Hah Hah.**

Let your voice shake.

Continue bouncing until you feel open.

18. Larger Movement I

Bounce up and down gently, saying your name.

Let your voice shake.

Continue bouncing, and try to stop your voice from shaking. The goal is to recognize tension.

Begin again, letting your voice shake.

19. Larger Movement II

Jump up and down gently, saying **Hah Hah Hah.**

Go through the entire range of your voice, from your lowest notes to your top note, continuing to jump on **Hah Hah Hah.**

Let your voice shake.

Stand still and go through the entire range again, saying **Hah Hah Hah.** Keep your neck and jaw relaxed as you go up into your high range.

Your voice doesn't shake, but stays connected. Let the voice crack. It doesn't matter. Just keep the body released.

Repeat a few times.

20. Finale

Bounce up and down, fling yourself around in a swirl, or roll around on the floor. Do any physical movement that feels free and loose.

At the same time, act a speech. Your voice will shake mightily.

Alternate acting while moving and acting while standing still. See if you maintain the emotional connection.

A BRIEF REMINDER

Once you are totally familiar with the daily workout, all you will need is this reminder for the correct sequence:

Body Alignment

1. Neck Release: Drop your head.

2. Curling Over: Roll all the way down your spine, and curl back up.

The Vocal Passageway

3. Tongue Exercise: Stretch

4. Big Yawn (soft palate)

5. Whispered Keh (soft palate and tongue)

6. Ngah Ngah (soft palate and tongue)

7. Tongue Relaxer: Tongue on lower lip

8. Jaw I, Relaxation: Gently move your jaws.

9. Jaw II, Isometric: Push your fist against your jaws in four positions.

Connecting Voice to Breath

10. Centering: Feel your breath in your abdomen.

11. Sound Vibration: Connect an unformed sound to your breath.

The Resonating Chambers

12. Chest

13. Hard Palate

14. The Sinuses

15. The Nose

16. The Skull

Liberating the Voice

17. Knees Only: Bounce gently with knees only.

18. Larger Movement I

19. Larger Movement II

20. Finale: The big roll-around

9

CONNECTING YOUR VOICE TO YOUR EMOTIONAL LIFE

The whole point of modern voice training is to connect the voice to the actor's emotional life. The voice is not "technical" work for the actor, but is an intimate, natural part of what he or she is feeling and expressing. When the voice is released on the breath, there is a corresponding emotional release as well.

This chapter provides you with three special exercises that should be approached after you have become familiar with the daily workout presented in the preceding chapter. These exercises may feel very technical at first, but if you persevere, the results can be quite effective and the exercises will show you how to be more honest.

Accordingly, the following work best if the text you use has personal meaning for you.

EXERCISE 1

Choose the first line of any speech from any scene, preferably one you are working on in a class or preparing for performance.

Imagine that the sound you are going to make is coming from the belly. Make a **Huh** sound.

Now, say the first word of your text, matching the pitch of the **Huh**. Remember, the sound is coming from your belly.

After the first word, allow your voice to go anywhere it needs to go to express the remainder of the line.

Repeat this procedure with each successive line of the speech; start with **Huh**, and then match the first word of the line.

Notice how starting each line with **Huh** puts your voice in a freer place.

Practice this for twenty minutes a day for a few weeks. If you have success, then only *think* the **Huh** sound and match the first word.

For most people, the sound will start in the lower half of the voice. This exercise is especially useful for women who tend to avoid the lower half of their voices.

When first tapping any previously unused portion of your vocal tract, your voice may sound dull to you. However, anyone listening to you hears an impressive vocal and emotional feedback. Actors often say they feel "blank" when they first try this exercise. Using the voice in a new way usually feels wrong at first. However, it doesn't sound wrong.

Continue to repeat and experiment with this exercise until it begins to feel comfortable.

The next two exercises are even more unusual in approach and have a startling impact when correctly executed. These exercises put you directly in touch with your feelings. You will discover what it feels like to actually *use* an emotionally connected voice.

EXERCISE 2

First, select a piece of material you like and feel connected to. It may be prose, poetry, or a speech from a play.

Now begin the exercise: Close your eyes and ask yourself, "What am I feeling?" Often you are feeling many different things. You do not have to *label* the emotion(s) you feel, although you may. The important thing is to try to get in touch with whatever you are feeling, even if it seems wrong for this particular speech.

Open your eyes and go to the text. Think the thoughts that are in the text and say the speech out loud—but try to stay in touch with your original feeling.

This may feel like tapping your head with one hand and rubbing your stomach with the other. Don't worry, and don't be concerned about being appropriate or correct. This exercise allows you to be vocally open, even if what you are feeling is absurd for the text (by that I mean it would be absurd to play a happy Hamlet or a joyful Medea). This feeling of being connected to your own emotions (and having an open instrument) can help you be an honest actor. For if you are open emotionally and instrumentally, and you are dealing with the thought "to be or not to be," you will be affected emotionally and you will act effectively.

Most actors doing this exercise are certain that the result could never be appropriate for actual performance. Surprisingly, this isn't always the case. Others often say how believable and interesting the result is. The reason is that several layers of emotions are being expressed, rather than one obvious emotion. This is what is going on with actors who are said to be "interesting," even when they aren't chewing the scenery. If you are connected to what you are feeling, and if your voice is released, the thoughts from the text will influence your emotional life. You will be effective.

Recognizing What You Are Feeling

Some actors have trouble with the beginning of exercise 2, above, in which you are supposed to identify what you are feeling. Some say, "I can't tell what I'm feeling," or "I feel nothing." An actor can't afford to be that unaware. If you cannot recognize, at least to some extent, what you are feeling at any given moment, you have to work to develop that ability. This is what I refer to as "getting in touch with your emotions." In other words, being aware that you have feelings and having some sense of what they are. Usually, people trained from childhood not to express emotion have learned to block out feelings. Part of the actor's job is to express emotion, and if you are cut off from your own feelings you will have to do some serious work on yourself.

Several good techniques can help you get in touch with your emotions, but I prefer the direct approach. If you are alive, you have emotions. I tell my students to ask themselves at least ten times throughout the day, "What am I feeling?" If you really do that, eventually you will have answers.

The answers do not have to be profound. You do not have to experience primal rage or joy. The answer can be many different things, from simple to complex, trivial to profound. Sometimes you can't label it, but you can sense it.

The purpose of the technique is to learn to be open when you choose to be. You may have some resistance at first, but you can get in touch with yourself. I've seen it done many times.

EXERCISE 3

This exercise takes the previous exercise one step further.

Sometimes actors make an intellectual choice concerning a character—he or she is strong or weak or shy or whatever. That doesn't mean they can skip making an emotional connection. This is an important part of the acting craft. If your instrument is responsive, you can easily react emotionally and vocally to a thought.

First, close your eyes. Release your belly. Breathe. Get in touch with your feeling, whatever it is.

Think this thought: "Stop this right now!" Stay with that thought, and your emotions will change in some way.

Now say the line out loud: "Stop this right now!" The new emotion will be expressed in your voice.

Students often say to me, "When I do this exercise, my voice doesn't come out the way I expected. It feels wrong. What should I do?" This is good, for the actor is telling me that he (or she) previously made an intellectual choice about interpretation and has left his emotional life and vocal instrument outside of the process. He assumed that sometime later he would be able to bring in voice and emotion. It won't work. The actor's performance will lack expression.

These are innovative and demanding exercises. They take real effort and concentration, but try them consistently and you will derive great results.

10

BREATHING IS A PART OF YOUR ACTING

Breathing is that part of expression that you as an actor must deal with from the very beginning of your preparation. It cannot be added on at the end. Yet I have been told countless times by directors and acting teachers that actors have to get to the emotional essence of the role without being "distracted by vocal technicalities."

I agree that when developing a role actors should not be distracted by technicalities, but breathing is most definitely not a technicality. Breathing is the core of life. The breath connects the actor to his or her emotion, and the voice conveys that emotion to the audience.

Observing the way a person is breathing is one of the ways we have of recognizing that individual's state of being. This automatically makes breathing a major component of the acting process.

For breathing to help you make the connection to emotional truth, it must be included from the beginning of your preparation—whether you are preparing a scene in class or rehearsing a play on Broadway. The last thing an actor needs is to go onstage or before the camera thinking about breathing, as if it were a new piece of information.

Breathing is connected not only to your emotional state, but also to your desire or need to say something and to the meaning of the words. I sometimes see actors get up to work in class and take a big deep breath, usually looking at the floor. Then they look at their partner. Then they start to talk. That big breath was connected to starting to act, rather than to what the actor wanted to express.

Understanding and opening up the breathing process—liberating the breath—allows the voice to reveal the character's inner emotional life. If you are breathing fully and if the breath is free, your voice will be personal and revealing.

LIBERATING THE BREATH

Human beings have found many bizarre ways to interfere with free and natural breathing. Corsets and girdles, breastplates and suits of armor, tights and belts—all these limit the depth and freedom of the breath. Moreover, we have also devised many unnatural "breathing techniques." Some teach the actor to breathe the same way with each breath, eliminating any variety or freedom in the breathing. Thus, almost every sound is the same, regardless of the content of the words, since the actor is working hard to breathe uniformly.

The truth is that an actor should breathe in response to the context of the situation, the meaning of the words, and the emotion being expressed. Ideally, the breath is free from external constraints and able to change freely all the time.

The basic secret of freeing the breath is this: If you release the lower abdominal muscles, the breath seems to go into your belly. (It doesn't, of course; in truth, it goes into your lungs.) Relaxing your abdomen, or belly, frees the diaphragm, the flat muscle that separates the abdomen from the chest cavity; in turn, your lungs are able to fill with as much air as you need. This is the natural way you breathe when you are sleeping.

If your abdominal muscles are released, the breath will automatically go into the lungs without effort. You don't need to push it there. Even if you need only a tiny amount of air, you still want to feel it start in the abdomen (rather than up in your chest). Likewise, if you need a lot of air, in order to be very loud or express a long thought, the breath goes first to the belly and continues up into the expanding rib cage.

Let's do an exercise to clarify this point.

Take a very large breath and then say "Hi." Now, release the rest of the breath. This is a forced way to breathe; it feels quite unnatural. Obviously, you don't need all that breath to just say "Hi." If you simply release your abdominal muscles, you will automatically take in as much air as you need.

Let's do another quick exercise.

Imagine that you are out on the street and you see a friend about to walk in front of a moving truck. You want to shout "Stop!" Go ahead, shout it now.

If you called out "Stop!" in a way to save your friend, I'm sure you didn't first say to yourself: "Large breath, now yell 'Stop!'" The point is, you don't have to consciously think about how much air to take in. It's an automatic response. You will automatically take in the correct amount to express the thought—that is, if you don't physically interfere with the natural process.

Knowing Where to Breathe in a Speech

Actors ask me where they should take a breath in a given speech. You can take a breath at any point the thought changes. (It's not usually a good idea to breathe according to punctuation.) If you are in touch with what you are saying, and if you can keep your abdominal muscles relaxed, chances are your breathing will be perfect—that is, your breathing will become part of what you are expressing and also tell us something about the character.

INCREASING LUNG CAPACITY

Actors are often taught to speak a certain number of lines on one breath, so they will be able to do long speeches without taking a breath. This is an old voice-training idea, involving endless counting exercises to see how far you can get on one breath. Basically, what it produces is a big voice that can count.

Another counterproductive exercise is the so-called rib reserved breathing, whereby the actor is taught to hold the rib cage expanded, which provides some additional resonance. Unfortunately, this method creates great physical tension and separates the voice from the inner emotional life and thought. The resulting voice tends to sound very announcer-like, devoid of emotion. This technique also creates a stiff, inexpressive body.

Still another method used to train actors to produce more sound is by "punching" the abdominal muscles. In this exercise, the actor is usually asked to count or say **Huh** over and over again—the sound being forcibly pushed out with the muscles of the abdomen. When you use muscle tension to push sound out, the voice cannot be emotionally revealing. Basically, the exercise connects the voice to the muscles, not the emotions. The sound you make is connected only to the violent muscular action.

Producing sound on the breath is the most expressive way to speak. Try these exercises now.

1. Take a breath, hold it in, and then say "Hello, how are you?" Now let the breath out. The expression is on the sigh at the end of the sentence.

2. Take a breath, let it out, and now say "Hello, how are you?" without taking another breath. The expression is on the sigh before you spoke the words. Thus, the words themselves are not very expressive or honest, because there is no breath underneath them.

3. This time, do not breathe at all before you say "Hello, how are you." There is no expression at all.

How, then, does an actor increase breath capacity? By physically stretching the muscles in the rib cage (by doing arm stretches) and by practicing saying long speeches in an emotionally connected manner.

REDUCING NERVOUSNESS

For thousands of years actors have tried to come up with reliable techniques to reduce or eliminate initial nervousness at the beginning of performances. One common method is to let out a long, slow, evenly controlled breath before the opening line. I call this *cooling out the breath.* Cooling out may be calming, but it dissipates emotions. When you "cool out" you are robbing yourself of your greatest gift, your ability to express emotion.

However, there is a way to reduce nervousness, yet retain emotional content: Instead of cooling out, simply start the text. You will feel more connected to the text, and soon your nervousness will subside.

BASIC RULES ON BREATHING

Breathing is very basic and natural, and I would simply impart these three basic rules for you to remember above all:

1. *Breathe through your mouth when you are speaking.* Breathing through your mouth is less contained and allows you to be more expressive. The breath goes to your lower abdomen first, and then up into the rib cage.

   Try this exercise: Say the line: "Hello, I'm glad to see you." Now take a very big breath through your nose and continue: "I'm glad I ran into you."

   Does it feel natural? Probably not.

   Now, do the same exercise, but this time breathe through your mouth. The phrase will be less held, much more natural, and more open.

2. *Free yourself up by letting go of physical tension and let the breath happen on its own.* Release the abdominal muscles and let the breath go there. (You don't need to manipulate your breath.)

3. *Take in only as much breath as you need to express the thought.* You want your breath to express your physical and emotional state. Little breaths for little thoughts; big breaths for big thoughts.

11

GETTING USED TO YOUR NEW SOUND

Even after you have successfully developed your vocal instrument a period of adjustment is almost always needed before you can actually use it in daily situations. This is awkward for everyone, and for some people it can be downright difficult.

For some lucky actors, however, the period of adjustment is smooth and wonderful. Some people are able to allow their developed voices into their lives and their acting quite easily, without any particular effort. This happens most often when the actor approves of the sound of his or her new vocal quality. "Strong" and "centered" are words I often hear.

They also notice a different response from people hearing them. I find this particularly true of women, but not exclusively. When you present yourself in a different way, obviously you are going to be heard in a different way and seen in a different way. And this is very interesting to many people. Not only do you change, but other people's perception of you also changes. In turn, you often find yourself changing more than you expected. Some people, for instance, had no idea they could have large voices.

Most people need to put some effort into actually using their newly developed voices. Just because the voice is developed doesn't mean you will use it. Vocal habits are strong. Most of us have grown up using our voices in limited ways, using only a part of our vocal range.

I tell my students that, to be effective vocally when acting, they must use their voices fully and expressively *in daily life.*

There is a practical professional reason for saying this. You cannot say to a casting agent, "When I'm in front of the camera (or on the stage), my voice is quite different." The agent won't believe you.

More importantly, the way you use the voice in daily life is part of your professional image, the impression you make when you first meet a casting person or a director. In this country, we tend to type-cast. Your voice is a large part of type-casting. When taking an interview, the actor must sound as if he or she can play the part. In fact, the interview is usually how an actor gets an audition in the first place.

When you meet casting people and other important figures in the business, your voice must also sound natural and honest. That can help you be recognizable as a potentially fine actor. If you produce your acting voice like a rabbit out of a hat, you will be seen as phony and hard to cast.

There are schools where the actor is taught to be very theatrical vocally—and word gets around. Many casting people in Los Angeles will not see actors from those programs because they know their voices will be too theatrical and, thus, too impersonal and distancing for the film and television work being done there.

As an actor, you must use your newly developed voice all the time—in your life and in your work. Full integration is the goal. That being said, let me repeat that integrating the vocal changes you achieve during workouts into daily use does not happen automatically. Because you have strength in a particular muscle, or the ability to relax a particular muscle or to express a certain emotional quality, does not mean that you will automatically do it. If you develop a good, strong voice, if you can hear it and feel it, then you often have to fight for your right to use it. You must make a conscious effort to integrate your new vocal changes into your life. You have to *decide* to do it, and then practice doing it. This is what integration involves.

INTEGRATING VOCAL CHANGES BY RELEASING TENSION

To integrate vocal changes into your life and work means, first, becoming aware of the sources of tension, and, second, releasing the tension whenever it appears. There are four distinct types of tension, depending on the circumstances:

1. The physical tension you walk around with all the time. People have different habits, but the most common areas of physical tension involve the shoulders and abdomen. Some people hold their shoulders up or back, and their heads forward. Some tighten their bellies. Some people hunch their upper backs. Others clench their teeth, or sit with their legs twisted around each other. We have all kinds of tension-producing habits which affect voice production.

2. Tension that occurs when you are speaking in front of a group. Sometimes the voice becomes tighter, or deeper, or higher, or more wobbly.

3. Tensions while acting. Some people switch to a stagy voice. More often, nervousness creates tension that limits vocal production.

4. Finally, and most importantly, tensions that arise in circumstances in which you are trying to express intense emotion. It can happen when you are having a fight with your spouse or when you're in the midst of your big scene onstage. The voice often becomes much higher in pitch or extremely tight. It often comes out sounding like a squeak or a whine.

In each of these circumstances, you must become aware of what you are doing and what is happening in your body. As you do your daily vocal workout, you will learn more about your body and its influence on your voice. You will learn to release muscles governing vocal tension, which will then release the voice. Then, when you find yourself in the circumstances that alter the sound of your voice, you will be aware of what is happening in your body. Then, too, you will be able to consciously release the muscles causing vocal constraints. You will be able to accomplish this even when you are feeling very emotional or nervous.

Dealing with Common Problems

As an actor you must take responsibility for the condition of your instrument. It's not enough to say, "When I get emotional, my throat tightens up and my voice gets squeaky." Whatever happens to your voice when you get emotional is habit. You can change the involuntary reaction by developing your awareness and doing exercises on a regular basis.

As we've seen, it's usually not hard to figure out what is interfering with vocal production. Most problems can be traced to tension in the neck, jaw, and tongue, or to restricted breathing that disconnects the voice from the thought. Releasing specific parts of the body that govern the vocal instrument and learning to connect breathing to the emotion you are feeling will solve most of the problems.

If, at any given time, you experience a constrained vocal production, try to simply focus on these common limiting factors:

- Restricted breathing

- Lack of chest vibration

- Lack of sinus and nasal vibration

- Excessive neck tension

- Trying to manipulate the voice when acting or speaking

If you find that you experience any of these problems in performance, turn back to Chapter 8 and review the complete exercises carefully, concentrating on the ones which focus directly on your problem.

And remember: You have to do the exercises on a daily basis. You have to understand what you are doing and why.

And, finally, you really have to *want* your discoveries to work for you. This last is the key to success—really fighting to integrate the vocal changes you make into your work. You have a right to your own voice.

INDEX